Slugs
Friend *or* Foe?

Slugs
Friend or Foe?

Know your garden slugs
and learn to live with them

Dr. Hayley Jones

Contents

WELCOME TO SLUGDOM

Most people do not love slugs. Slugs (and snails) have been decried as a horticultural problem for centuries, and gardeners today still battle to preserve their hostas and lettuce. The distress of finding every one of a row of seedlings demolished may make you understandably displeased with slug-kind, and slugs feature highly in enquiries to the Royal Horticultural Society Gardening Advice service in the UK. Yet despite many products and recommendations and for their control, they persist in causing strife.

Slugs are, however, often understudied and misunderstood. In my near decade in the plant health team at the RHS, I have worked on finding sustainable ways for gardeners to manage slugs, trawling the literature, talking to a range of gardeners, and carrying out my own experiments. During this time, I've not only been fascinated by their biology but also learned about the unique and complex place they occupy in the garden ecosystem.

Not all slugs and snails are plant ravagers, and many, in fact, are beneficial in the garden, especially by helping to recycle dead material. Plus, even those that are deemed "bad" are a food source for many more charismatic and treasured garden animals, including birds, insects, and mammals. To add to the confusion, many slug species are both friend and foe, sometimes eating plants and at other times preferring the dead stuff. For this reason, the word "pest" is not always helpful, and labels such as this make it easier to attempt to eradicate an animal without appreciating the complexity of its place in the garden ecosystem.

Slugs seem to be much more strongly reviled than snails, with many people finding them unsurpassably revolting. Snails, despite being as culpable for plant nibbling, are often depicted as cute garden creatures, featuring in children's books and nature-themed artwork. Slugs appear much more rarely in cultural works, and when they do, they're mostly portrayed as something monstrous or disgusting. The shell seems to be key: it gives snails a wholesome, relatable feel, and, of course, means you can relocate them without having to touch the slimy part. People are much more likely to ask me "What's the point of...?" about slugs than about snails.

In this book, I aim to show you that the slug, as much as any creature, deserves not only to exist but also to be appreciated for its role in the ecosystem and for its fascinating features. I hope that once you get comfortable with them, you might be convinced to find their little tentacled faces cute, as I have!

This book will take you on a journey through slugdom, starting with their external features and inner workings (including their shells).

Next, we will venture into the garden to look at slug behavior and ecology, including the several places that slugs occupy in the garden food chain.

Once we discover that not all slugs are plant-eaters, and that some of them are actually helpful to gardeners, the next question is

Not all slugs and snails are plant ravagers, and many are beneficial in the garden.

The slug deserves to be appreciated for its role in the ecosystem and for its fascinating features.

always, "How can we tell which is which?" Slug identification is unfortunately much more difficult than for many other groups of animals, and it involves getting extremely close up and personal. Specialized identification guides are helpful for those who want to know precisely, and I strongly recommend the Field Studies Council's *Slugs of Britain and Ireland*, which is also helpful in the US. Here, I have synthesized the basics to get you started with slug ID, and have included profiles of 20 common garden slug species and a few rare and interesting ones.

Finally, there is a chapter on what you can do to minimize slug-feeding damage in your garden. I've answered so many sluggy questions through the RHS Gardening Advice service, or in any forum where my garden slug expertise comes up, and have also heard many tips and suggestions from experienced gardeners.

Unfortunately, the scientific literature has a lot of gaps on this topic because the majority of research is carried out (perhaps understandably) with crop farming in mind. Agricultural settings are very different from gardens in terms of what is practical and profitable. Many hands-on and homemade techniques will, therefore, be completely without published studies to draw on.

The advice here discusses whether there is scientific evidence for different techniques, but does not necessarily discount some of the less proven options. I cover the most slug-friendly options, progressing to the pros and cons of the more slug-lethal ones. This section will particularly focus on the cultural management (plant choice and care) and biological controls (natural predators and parasites) that are relevant, achievable, and sustainable for gardeners.

By the end, I hope you will feel more warmly toward and interested in slugs. That's not to say I expect you to let your patch become an unfettered slug haven. But I aim to impart appreciation and sympathy for slugs' intriguing biology and their position in the world, even when they're demolishing your dahlias.

Finally, if you want to delve more into the fascinating science of slugs, refer to the bibliography and resources on pp136–39.

RIGHT: A dark form of the leopard slug (see p76) climbs a horsetail stem.

BEYOND
THE GARDEN

While snails appear regularly in art, culture, and symbology, slugs are much less frequently depicted, but the garden isn't the only place humans interact with slugs.

Slugs and language
It seems likely that the word "slug" meant a slow or lazy person before it was applied to the subcategory of snails without an external shell, which is ironic considering they are speedier than snails, on average, perhaps due to their lack of a visible shell (see p14).

What are slugs and snails called around the world? In fact, not all languages have separate words for the visibly and invisibly shelled. Scots English, for example, uses the word "snail" for both slugs and snails; Italian has "*lumaca*" to denote both; and Portuguese uses "*lesma.*"

Slugs in art
Snails feature much more widely than slugs in art, with slugs mostly restricted to botanical or zoological illustrations. However, the earliest-known record of a recognizable slug in art is an oil painting of the visit of the Wise Men, part of a triptych by Dieric Bouts, from about 1454.

The presence of snails and slugs has symbolized various things in artworks, both positive and negative, but in religious paintings from this time, they are often used to represent sin, sloth, and immodesty.

In a series of illustrations entitled *The Flowers Personified* by J.J. Grandville (1847), the sensitive plant (*Mimosa pudica*) is depicted as a beautiful woman fearfully recoiling as she is being rapidly(ish) pursued by a slug.

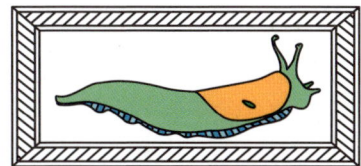

On the silver screen, the trailer for the 1988 horror film *Slugs* mentions them having "several rows of teeth," but we know the truth might be even more horrifying (see p36).

In 2018 at London's Tate Britain gallery, two enormous leopard slugs were installed crawling over the building's facade. They were truly impressive, and realistic, except for the illumination that the artist Monster Chetwynd used to great effect on their bodies and to depict slime trails over the building.

The University of California Santa Cruz has the banana slug (*Ariolimax* species) as its mascot. This became official in 1986, after six years of the student body campaigning that it wanted to be nicknamed "the slugs," not "the sea lions."

Slugs in technology

Leopard slugs were used as detectors for mustard gas during World War I (1914–18). The discovery was first made accidentally by Paul Bartsch, a scientist studying leopard slug mating habits (see p76), and he tested and transmitted this information to the Allied forces on the European front.

In Sweden, the large black slug (see p56) was traditionally used as a lubricant, especially for wheel axles. This was a common-enough practice that horse-drawn carts often had a *snigelkruk*, a tub to hold the slugs, and one dialect includes the verb "*att snigla,*" meaning "to slug," as a synonym for "to lubricate."

Slugs and snails were often used to represent sin, sloth, and immodesty in religious paintings.

What are gastropods?

SLUGS AND SNAILS

Slugs and snails are gastropods, a word based on the Greek "*gaster,*" meaning "stomach," and "*poda,*" which means "foot." This etymology is probably founded on them "walking" on their stomach, but is often used by gardeners to grumble about them being a walking stomach!

The gastropod group of animals is part of the phylum (larger group) of mollusks. They are characterized by a head with tentacles; a broad, flattened foot; and the back of the body at least partly covered by a mantle (see pp48–49).

How did slugs and snails evolve?
Slugs and snails are both descended from an ancestral gastropod that was like a snail with a coiled shell. For most animals you're probably familiar with, food goes in one end and out the other. But for snails, because the bulk of the body is inside the shell, the digestive tract goes from the mouth into the body, then loops round and back out of the shell.

Over evolutionary time, slugs appeared from among the snails as their shells shrank, but in most cases, this shell hasn't disappeared entirely. The majority of slugs you see in your garden have a small shell under the skin at the back of the mantle. For some species, it is like an oval fingernail, and in others, it is reduced to just some granules of calcium carbonate.

Slugs retain many elements of the snail ancestor's internal organ layout. For most slugs, this means the anus is located on their right-hand

Over evolutionary time, slugs appeared from among the snails as their shells shrank, but in most cases, this shell hasn't disappeared entirely.

side near their head. In fact, all the body openings are here, including the breathing pore and genital opening. Slugs still conform to the ancestor's internal asymmetrical, coiled body plan, despite their bodies looking pretty symmetrical when looked at from the top down.

What is a slug?

There are slightly varying definitions of a slug, but I prefer the one that encompasses all gastropods that cannot fit their body entirely into the shell. This includes the semi-slugs (see p100) that look quite snail-like, as well as the shelled slugs that have a small, plate-like shell still obvious on the outside of their bodies (see p96).

The broad variation in slug body and shell types is because slugs have evolved several times separately from snail ancestors. This means some of the slug families are not closely related, despite similarity in overall body form—this is known as convergent evolution. The key features of four prominent slug families are outlined on pp50–53.

Why be a slug, rather than a snail?

Not having a portable home seems like a downgrade, but there must be perks, or else slugs wouldn't have kept appearing in evolutionary time among the snails.

One benefit is the ability to squeeze into small spaces, and slugs make great use of this to go underground, hiding from hot and dry conditions and above-ground predators, and, in some cases, living and feeding in a subterranean lifestyle.

Another benefit of a reduced shell is a lower calcium requirement, and this has enabled slugs to colonize a wider range of habitats.

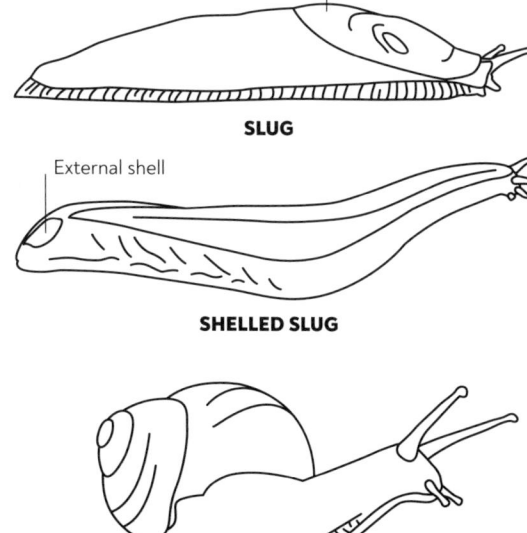

Internal shell

SLUG

External shell

SHELLED SLUG

SNAIL

Gastropod variation
Slugs can have a small internal or external shell, while snails have a full-sized external shell.

LIFE CYCLE

The biology and behavior of slugs is as fascinating as it is complicated. Here's an overview.

The best of both worlds

Slugs are hermaphrodite, which means that they have both male and female reproductive organs. So when two individuals mate, both can be fertilized and go on to lay their own eggs. The intricate anatomy that allows this includes a single gonad, which produces the initial cells that later differentiate into eggs and sperm. These elaborate reproductive organs provide many of the features used to identify species that otherwise look very similar on the outside.

Slugs also can self-fertilize, and therefore are able to reproduce even if no mates are available. This may be a great benefit, enabling an enterprising single slug to start a whole new population in a previously unclaimed territory.

However, self-fertilization is not without hazards because, as with other forms of inbreeding, it can lead to an accumulation of harmful genes. Plus, a population with little genetic diversity is more at risk from environmental changes and extreme events. Despite this, self-fertilization is the preferred means of reproduction for many species of slugs.

Timing is everything

Many slugs in temperate US regions have a year-long life cycle. Most slugs lay eggs in spring or fall, juveniles grow to adulthood throughout the summer, and then adults mostly hide underground over winter, ready to start the cycle again and dying off not long after.

Some species fast-track this process, such as the gray field slug (see opposite and p88), which can have two or more generations in a year, with each individual able to

Self-fertilization is the preferred means of reproduction for many species of slugs.

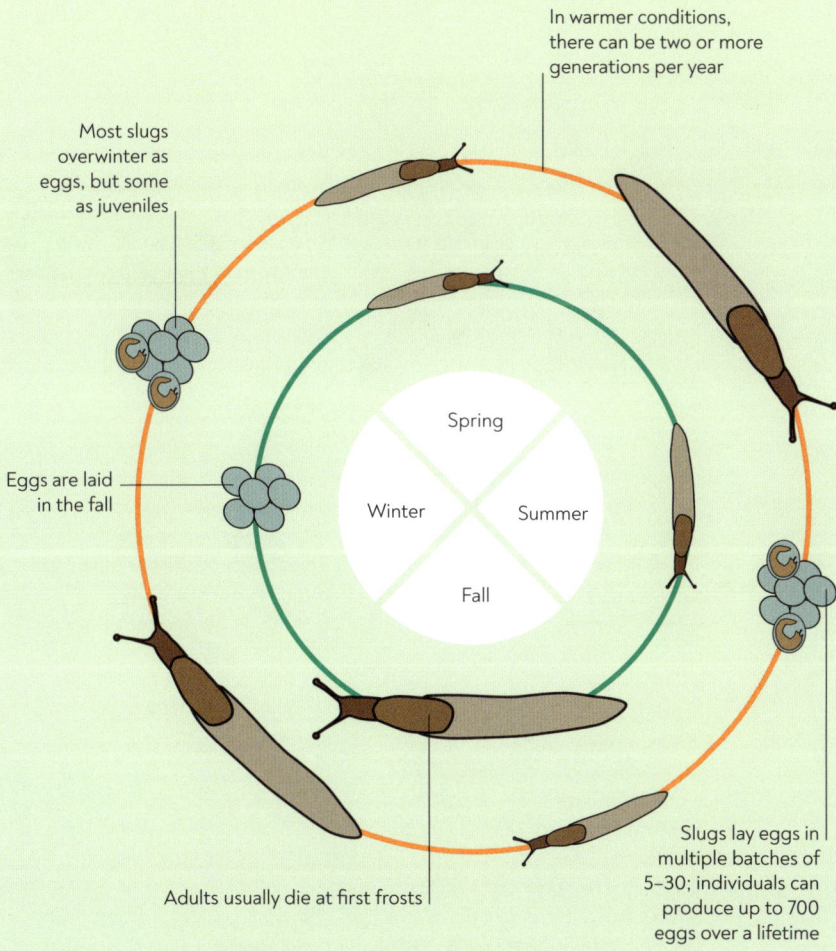

Gray field slug life cycle
Depending on climatic conditions, gray field slugs (*Deroceras reticulatum*) can have one or two generations a year.

— Warmer weather
— Cooler weather

In warmer conditions, there can be two or more generations per year

Most slugs overwinter as eggs, but some as juveniles

Eggs are laid in the fall

Spring

Winter   Summer

Fall

Adults usually die at first frosts

Slugs lay eggs in multiple batches of 5–30; individuals can produce up to 700 eggs over a lifetime

The gray field slug is able to produce up to 700 eggs in its life span.

each other, creating a rather beautiful circular symmetry.

Next, the slugs project a special appendage to stroke the partner as the circling continues, sometimes for more than an hour. This stimulates the partner to get ready for mating. Eventually, both individuals turn out their genitalia into the space between them and interlock. Droplets of sperm are exchanged, and the slugs soon go their separate ways.

Other groups of slugs vary somewhat in the use of appendages and other details of mating—for example, the more dramatic exploits of the leopard slug (see p76).

A few days after their romantic encounter, both slugs are ready to lay their eggs, although many species will hold on to sperm until a suitable time for egg-laying. The parental slugs dig a small hole and lay their eggs inside, which can hatch after one to two weeks.

Slug eggs are usually small white or translucent pearls, but the cellar slugs (see pp80, 82) have lemon-shaped eggs.

produce up to 700 eggs in its lifespan (12 months or more in temperate regions of the US).

At the other end of the scale, some slugs in the Limacidae family (see p53), such as the leopard slug (see p76), can live several years.

Making babies

Slug courtship is often elaborate and sometimes very complicated indeed. The version the Agriolimacidae family of slugs (see p53) follows goes like this.

First, the slug must find a partner, often by encountering a mucus trail, sensing that it belongs to a suitable partner of the same species, and following it to find them. The pair start to circle around and around

ABOVE LEFT: Slugs develop inside eggs, with newly hatched juveniles roaming nearby.

RIGHT: Two *Arion* slugs circle around each other as they mate.

SLUG FACTS!

~87 slug species in the US

~1,200 terrestrial gastropod species in the US

74,000+ worldwide gastropod species

SLUGS BY NUMBERS

1 shell

1 foot

1 lung

4 tentacles

2,000–8,000 teeth covering their tongue-like radula

1 sex—all are hermaphrodite

Up to 100 or more eggs per batch, depending on the species

Slug diversity

It's estimated there are 5,000 species of slugs worldwide, and almost 70,000 species of snails (land and aquatic).

There are approximately 85–90 slug species in the US. US gastropod species number in the 1,200s.

Slug sizes

Slugs in the US vary in size enormously, from the banana slug, which reaches 10¼in (26cm) in length, to the introduced hedgehog slug, at only ¾in (2cm) long.

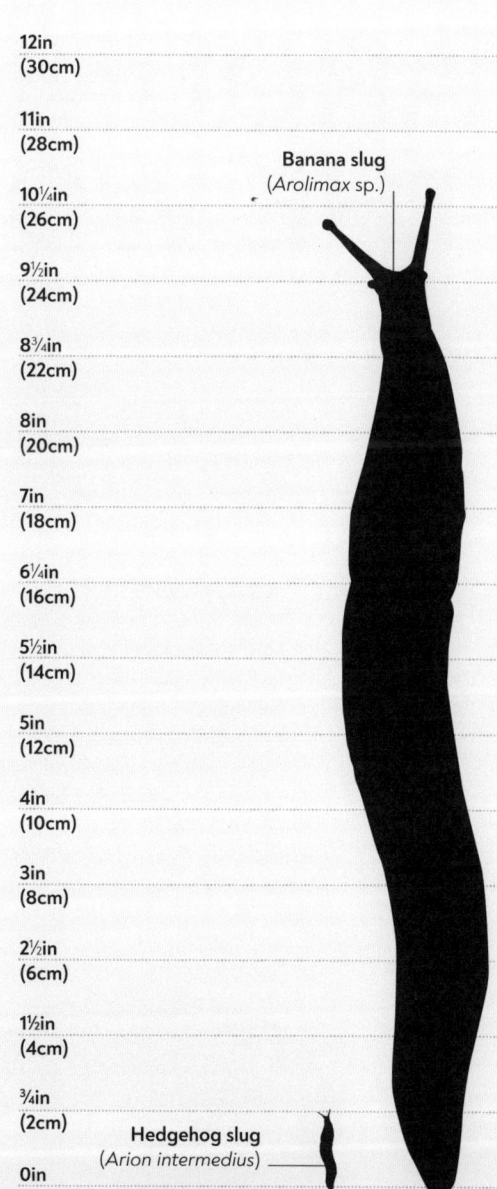

Banana slug
(*Arolimax* sp.)

12in
(30cm)

11in
(28cm)

10¼in
(26cm)

9½in
(24cm)

8¾in
(22cm)

8in
(20cm)

7in
(18cm)

6¼in
(16cm)

5½in
(14cm)

5in
(12cm)

4in
(10cm)

3in
(8cm)

2½in
(6cm)

1½in
(4cm)

¾in
(2cm)

Hedgehog slug
(*Arion intermedius*)

0in

Size (and speed) matters

The biggest US slug is the banana slug (*Arolimax* sp.), which can grow up to 10¼in (26cm) long. The smallest introduced slug in the US is the hedgehog slug (*Arion intermedius*), with a maximum length of ¾in (2cm).

The fastest slug in the UK is the tramp slug (*Deroceras invadens*), which has been recorded reaching speeds of 57½ft (17.6m) per hour/ 11½in (29.4cm) per minute/¼in (4.9mm) per second.

SLUGS AROUND THE WORLD

Let's get a global perspective on the group of gastropods known as slugs. There are about 5,000 species in the world, with enormous variety in their appearance, behavior, and worldwide distribution.

Snazzy slugs

Most slugs are fairly dark, dull, and camouflaged with the ground they live in, but there are a couple of notable exceptions.

The Pacific banana slug (five species including *Ariolimax columbianus*) is large, up to 10¼in (26cm) in length, and comes in a range of colors, with the most memorable being a striking yellow with black spots on the tail. It is found in the humid coastal forests of northwest US and Canada. As well as its amazing colors, it is famous for its habit of gnawing off its partner's penis after mating.

The Kaputar pink slug is really hot pink, and incredibly rare and special. Its scientific name hasn't been confirmed yet—it's known as *Triboniophorus* sp. nov. 'Kaputar' ("sp. nov." is short for the Latin "new species"). The slug is only known from a single location at the summit of an extinct volcano, Mount Kaputar, in New South Wales, Australia. Its hot-pink color may be to camouflage it with fallen snow gum leaves, but we won't know for sure until more studies have been completed.

Kaputar pink slug
The Kaputar pink slug is found on a single mountaintop in Australia. Scientists are investigating whether its amazing color is camouflage with fallen *Eucalyptus* leaves.

Spreading slugs

Of the estimated 74,000-plus gastropod species in the world, the 5,000 or so species of slugs make up less than 7 percent. They are much more numerous in temperate regions, and in the rainy UK, slugs make up 27 percent of the terrestrial gastropods compared to 15–20 percent in continental northwest Europe.

When the Europeans colonized other parts of the world, they (accidentally) took many of their slugs along for the ride. Increasing global movement in the past century has continued to introduce species into new regions, especially temperate ones such as Japan, New Zealand, Canada, and the US.

Many European slug species have become established in the US, and some have become particularly problematic for farmers and gardeners. These include the gray field slug (see p88), the blue-black soil slug (see p64), and the large red slug (see p56).

Suffering slugs

Not all slugs are successfully storming the world. The Kaputar pink slug is endangered because its habitat is so specific, a high-altitude forest in Australia. Similarly, the Kerry slug (see p70) is found in only two

Many color forms exist, but yellow with black splotches is the most iconic

The Pacific banana slug
Named for its yellow colouring, the Pacific banana slug is found in northwest America.

places in the world, west and southwest Ireland, and northwest Portugal and Spain. Happily, the Kerry slug story shows some globally joined-up thinking as it has protection plans in Ireland, even though it is not endangered there but is declining in its only other region.

Endemic species (those that are only present in a particular place) are most at risk in a changing world. Loss or fragmentation of wild habitat, invasive predators, and pollution could hit these species more severely than others. Slugs that are associated with human habitats are less likely to suffer, but the effects of climate change could still be huge because our slimy friends are so weather dependent.

The effects of climate change could be huge for slugs because they are so weather dependent.

Your garden
ecosystem

SLUGS IN THE GARDEN

Slugs are present in most gardens, and although we do see evidence of their presence from their slime trails and nibbles on our plants, we don't always see them going about their business.

Underground movers

As we've seen, the lack of a shell gives slugs great freedom of movement. They can squeeze through cracks, pores, and earthworm burrows to travel fairly easily underground. That is why you don't see the vast numbers of slugs that inhabit your garden—they have a very handy hiding spot.

As far as abundance goes, the press often cites 200 slugs per 11 square feet (1 sq m) in the UK (and likely similar for temperate US regions), but this is the upper limit of what studies show. In your garden, it's probably more in the range of 50–100 slugs per 11 square feet.

Night and day

Slugs are mostly active at night to avoid one of their greatest enemies, the sun. Their bodies are prone to drying out, and so the weather plays a huge part in their well-being and success (see p30). For that reason, they follow a mostly nocturnal lifestyle.

DAY

Most slugs shelter underground or in the leaf litter during the day.

NIGHT

Slugs can come up to the surface at nighttime without the risk of drying out.

Most slugs live in the leaf litter and top few inches of the soil but can go down below 4in (10cm) fairly easily.

Subterranean species such as the shelled slugs (see p96) and Milacidae (see p50) can go much deeper, but usually stay at a depth of around 12in (30cm).

Slugs are able to make the most of any warm spells to pop up and feed if the opportunity presents itself.

The timing of peak slug activity during the night seems to vary by species. The gray field slug (see p88), for instance, gets going as soon as the sun sets; the yellow cellar slug (see p80), shortly after; and the Budapest keeled slug (see p72), not until midnight.

Some slugs are still active after the sun comes up, including many of the *Arion* slugs. The larger *Arion* slugs (see p56), in particular, are often seen out in the daytime, and for that reason, they tend to be on the receiving end of a lot of gardeners' wrath. Then they all tuck themselves away before the midday heat.

Hot and cold

Slugs are ectothermic—that is, they have a body temperature that varies with their surroundings—and need conditions to be above a certain temperature to be active. In the winter, they hide out in their underground homes, insulated from most frost, and wait for the spring.

Unlike snails, which seal themselves inside their shells and therefore stay truly dormant, slugs are able to make the most of any warm spells to pop up and feed if the opportunity presents itself. We saw a stark example of this during the Slugs Count project (see pp44–45),

when one participant found active slugs making the most of a warmer wall when there was snow on the ground.

In the hottest and driest parts of summer, slugs also remain hidden underground, and they are primed to resume activity when the rains come.

Climate change

Being so connected to the weather means that slugs are bound to be impacted by climate changes: warmer and wetter weather is likely to benefit them, but an increasing occurrence of drought could have a negative effect on their populations.

SLIME TRAILS

Slugs are famous for their sticky slime, and it definitely contributes to people finding them revolting, but this slime (or mucus) serves many important purposes.

Movement and inertia

The mucus on the foot of a slug lubricates its movement over all kinds of terrain. It also helps it to squeeze through tiny pores in the soil when it is traveling underground. The slime trail left behind is mostly water, with about 10 percent made up of carbohydrates, proteins, and other materials. These elements give the mucus some remarkable physical properties: it is more solid and adhesive when the slug is stationary, and becomes more liquid when the foot exerts pressure to move forward.

Bioengineering scientists at Imperial College London and Harvard University were inspired by the slime of the dusky slug (see p62) to invent a new medical glue.

Hydration

The nature of slug and snail skin means they are vulnerable to drying out. This is particularly important for slugs compared to snails, as they have no handy shelter to retreat inside and preserve their water.

Their slime covers and protects their body, but the water it contains gradually evaporates. They need to seek shelter if it is dry, hot, or windy and replenish their water, usually by eating, but they can also absorb water through their skin. Small slugs suffer from drying out more quickly than larger slugs because of their large surface area compared to their size. That is why big slugs are more likely to be seen out and about.

Protection

As well as protecting them from the weather, the mucus can protect slugs from other threats. Many predators are deterred by the slime, but you may see a blackbird wiping a slug

TOP The route a slug has taken can often be seen by the mucus trail it leaves behind.

ABOVE Watery mucus evaporates away with barely a trace, but thicker slime, as here, is longer lasting.

LEFT Slugs produce slime from several places on their body. *Arion* slugs, such as this one, have a large mucus pore on the tail tip.

For a potential romantic couple, sampling the mucus of the partner is a key step in courtship.

on the grass to get the excess off before consuming. Certain species produce more watery mucus to make themselves slippery, and others have slime that tastes more unpalatable in response to attack.

Slug slime can also protect from hazardous substances, especially externally, when the slug produces extra mucus to shed the material. When exposed to internal or external poisons, such as slug pellets or salt, slugs continually produce mucus to try to shed it. This means that dehydration is often the main cause of death. Not a good way to go!

Following the trail

Slugs smell and taste the slime trails they come across using their tentacles. They can recognize their own signature trail, helping them return to their preferred resting place underground or under a pot, or their favorite feeding spot. If they encounter a stranger's slime trail, they can detect whether it belongs to the same species as themselves.

For a potential romantic couple, sampling the mucus of the partner is a key step in courtship. Slime then has an important role in the act itself, with some species producing a mucus platform to mate on, and others the more elaborate mucus rope (see leopard slug, p76).

You may have been puzzled by the presence of a slime trail (especially inside the house) and tried to follow it toward the culprit, only to find the trail mysteriously ends. That's another example of the magic of slug mucus and slugs' ability to modify its composition. If the slug starts producing a very watery slime en route, it will evaporate away, leaving no discernible trail.

Testing slime
As well as leaving a slime trail behind, slugs can smell and taste trails they encounter to see if they belong to a potential mate.

WHAT DO SLUGS EAT?

Slugs eat everything! They have a very broad range of diets and include herbivores, detritivores, and carnivores. Some species have specializations and preferences, and others eat a huge diversity of foods, so slugs span every level of the food chain.

Who eats what?

There are lots of unknowns in the diets of slugs, especially their real preferences rather than what they will eat if necessary. In captivity, slugs often accept food such as lettuce or carrots, even if these aren't something they would usually eat in the wild.

While lab studies of feeding preference can't always be extrapolated to the garden, a few scientists in the 20th century spent a lot of time offering different foods to slugs, giving us an essential insight into these otherwise elusive nocturnal creatures.

Herbivores

Gobbling your veggies, demolishing your hostas, and nibbling your potatoes are what slugs are famous for. The gray field slug and some other slugs in the Agriolimacidae family (see p53) are the major culprits here, as live plant material is their food of choice, and this brings them into frequent conflict with farmers and gardeners. Herbivores don't always clash with humans, though; some slug species prefer mosses, liverworts, or weedy wild plants.

Herbivores don't always clash with humans; some slug species prefer mosses, liverworts, or weedy wild plants.

Detritivores

Detritus (dead material) is softer and easier to rasp at (see p36) than living material, so it's not surprising that many slugs prefer it. The fungivores and algae feeders are incorporated in this group for ease. Most of the limacid slugs (see p53) refuse live plants, or only lightly nibble a few of them, but are more enthusiastic about fungal foodstuffs. Many slugs eat animal waste too, including carrion and feces, which makes them important for nutrient recycling in the garden ecosystem and general clean-up.

Carnivores

At the top of the food chain, carnivore slugs don't wait until their prey has died to taste meat. This diet is more rare, perhaps because slugs aren't so good at the chase part of hunting! The *Testacella* shelled slugs (see p96) and the spookily named ghost slug (see p98) have a specialized diet of earthworms.

Cannibalism is also not unheard of in slugs, sometimes in the *Testacella* slugs, while the *Arion* slugs are also happy to eat their erstwhile friends, especially in captivity.

Omnivores

Very many slugs fall into this "eats anything" category, even when they have preferences. The *Arion* slugs, for example, are superbly omnivorous, with several species able to feed on live and dead plant material, animal waste, dead slugs, other dead animals, fungi, algae, lichen, and more. An example of these is the large red slug (see p56), which is regularly seen eating both dog food and dog poop—the pinnacle of efficiency!

HOW DO SLUGS EAT?

Have you ever looked a slug in the face? They have marvelous mouthparts to help them feed, as well as lots of special senses. The upper tentacles where the eyes are have olfactory sensors, so they can use them to smell.

Detecting and tasting food
Slugs can use the sensors to detect potential foods from a distance and move toward them. The leopard slug (see p76) has been shown to be able to sense and move toward food from at least 6½ft (2m) away. However, many slugs, such as the gray field slug (see p88), don't seem to use long-distance sensing and simply roam around until they encounter food by chance.

The hungry slug will then use all four tentacles to touch, taste, and decide if the object is food. Next, they can turn out their lips to taste the food more sensitively and judge whether it is good to eat.

Remarkable radula
Instead of biting with teeth or jaws, slugs graze using their radula—a tongue-like organ covered in thousands of tiny teeth. Slugs push it forward out of their mouth and drag it back in over the food surface, like a cheese grater, scraping little bits into their mouth. You can see the pattern of this rasping radula in the markings on algae-covered greenhouse panes.

Choosy creatures
Although many species are omnivorous, this doesn't mean slugs will carelessly eat anything they come across. Even though they will or can eat many things, they seem to have favorite foods.

The criteria they use to choose their favorites aren't completely understood, but probably combine elements that make food attractive, like a high starch content, and those that do the opposite, like plant-defense chemicals. Many plants contain or can produce chemicals that are deterrents to slug feeding, including silicon, latex, tannins, alkaloids, and cyanide preludes.

The selective feeding of slugs, especially on seedlings, means that they help shape which plants are present or dominant in their habitats, and this can actually lead to overall greater plant diversity.

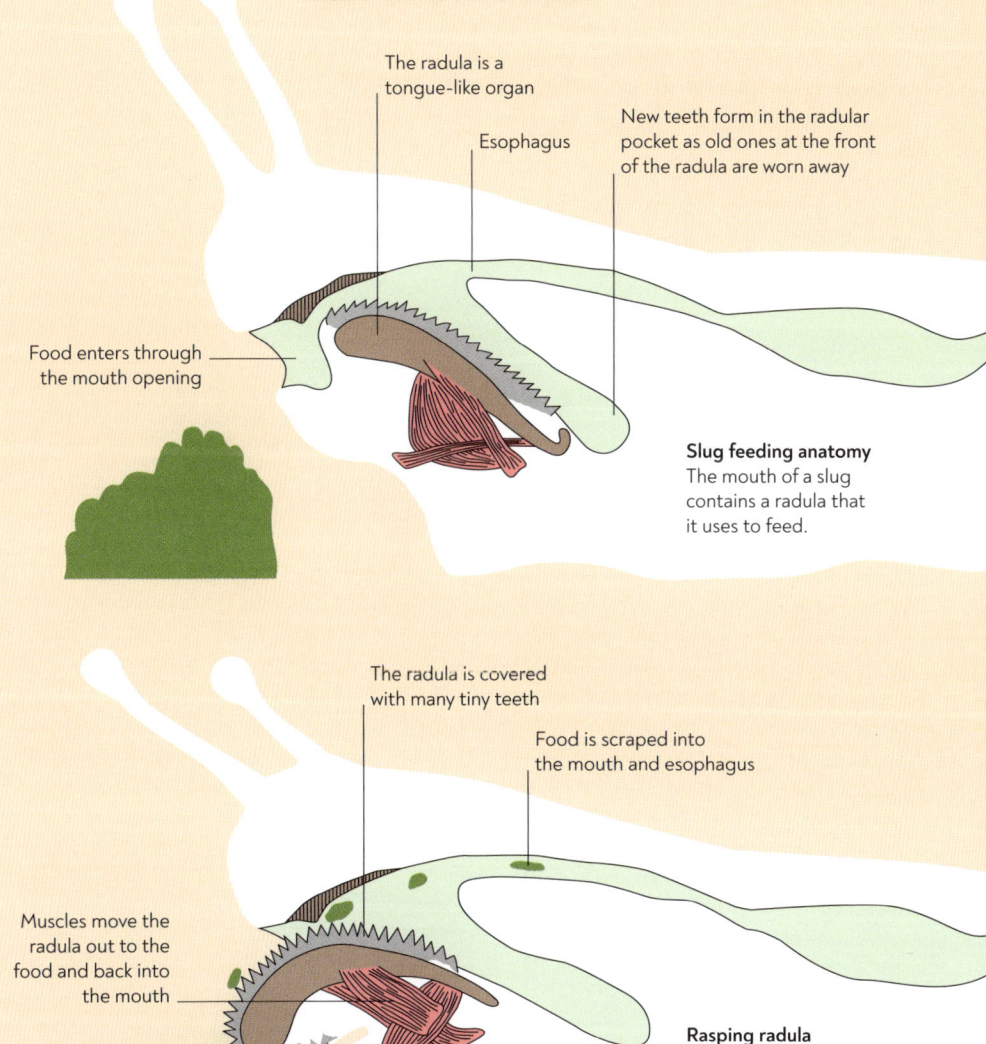

INSIDE THE MOUTH OF A SLUG

The radula is a tongue-like organ

Esophagus

New teeth form in the radular pocket as old ones at the front of the radula are worn away

Food enters through the mouth opening

Slug feeding anatomy
The mouth of a slug contains a radula that it uses to feed.

The radula is covered with many tiny teeth

Food is scraped into the mouth and esophagus

Muscles move the radula out to the food and back into the mouth

Rasping radula
A slug feeds by pushing out its radula and scraping it back over the food to drag small pieces into its mouth.

WHO EATS SLUGS?
Big predators

The thought might make you feel rather queasy, but plenty of other animals find slugs to be a tasty treat, including mammals, birds, amphibians, and reptiles.

Shrews and other mammals
Common warm-blooded slug predators in the US and some of its overseas islands and territories include at least nine species of shrews, two species of squirrels, two species of mice, two species of rats, and also chipmunks and skunks.

Other mammals that eat slugs include badgers, foxes, and moles, but slugs aren't often their favorite food; they eat them only when their preferred foods are scarce. We might think that the very big jaws of badgers would make short work of slugs, but they are only a very small percent of badgers' diet—they prefer insects, earthworms, and frogs—but that small percentage is still a lot of slugs in places where badgers are numerous.

Birds
Many US birds have been recorded as eating slugs, including northern cardinals, grouse, wild turkeys, and blackbirds. A notable few rank slugs as a favorite food, including song thrushes and starlings. The starling likes its slugs juicy and will pick out larger individuals of the gray field slug (see p88) rather than small ones.

Some birds actively seek out snails as a source of nutritional calcium for egg-laying, but it's not clear whether they can also get their calcium from slugs.

A few birds rank slugs as a favorite food, including song thrushes and starlings.

ABOVE A slowworm feeds on a large slug.

LEFT A starling has captured a slug, one of its favorite foods, in its beak.

Amphibians and reptiles

Salamanders, toads, and turtles are reportedly fond of eating slugs, perhaps because they are similarly slimy creatures, so they aren't deterred by the mucus. However, what proportion of their diet is made up of slugs and snails doesn't seem to have been measured.

Slowworms are voracious slug-eaters in the UK and consume many types of slugs, but they prefer the smooth eating experience of the gray field slug to the very sticky large red slug (see p56).

European snakes don't appear to have any particular penchant for slugs, but there are several species of slug-eating snakes in North America.

Domestic animals

Ducks and chickens are known to gobble down slugs quite readily, with perhaps a little mucus-induced reluctance, and a flock can make short work of several slugs. Chickens scratch the soil as part of their feeding routine, and so they are able to turn up slugs and other hidden creatures. Like slugs, ducks and chickens are omnivorous, so your garden plants are not necessarily safe in their company, either.

Pigs, while they mostly eat plant material, are omnivorous, and they have been known to eat slugs and snails. Like chickens, they are very capable of rooting them out of the top layers of soil as they feed, using their snout.

WHO EATS SLUGS?
Small predators

The most formidable slug-eaters are actually those in slugs' own weight class: invertebrate predators.

Ground beetles

This is a big group of beetles known scientifically as the Carabidae family, with at least 40,000 species worldwide and 2,500 in the US. Ground beetles can eat lots of different types of prey, but it has been shown, at least for some species, that they will actively seek out large slugs to hunt and can even keep slug populations measurably in check.

Some are more adapted to slug eating, such as the violet ground beetle (*Carabus violaceus*), which overcomes the slugs' mucus-producing defense by administering a rapid bite to the back of the head. They are probably the most numerous slug predators in farms, gardens, and wild spaces.

Fireflies

These famously luminescent creatures are actually a family of beetles, Lampyridae. Both male and female beetles glow, but the adult female glows much more noticeably in order to attract a mate.

It is the faintly glowing larvae that are the predators, and unlike most of the other invertebrate predators, these are specialists, feeding exclusively on slugs and snails. They bite their prey with their jaws, which are adapted

to inject paralyzing digestive juices, allowing them to take down prey bigger than themselves.

Fireflies are sadly in decline, probably due to the effects of habitat loss, climate change, and light pollution.

Sciomyzid flies

Known as marsh flies or snail-killing flies, this family has around 540 species worldwide, with the vast majority of species feeding exclusively on gastropods. They are particularly fascinating because they use both predation and parasitism in their life cycle.

European species *Tetanocera elata*, for example, hatch from eggs, and the larvae enter *Deroceras* slugs through the slugs' mucus-producing gland on the front of the foot. They spend their first two larval stages as parasitoids, living inside the slug's body, feeding on it, and growing until eventually the slug is killed. Once the slug has died, they leave the body and become predators, consuming four to nine additional slugs to complete their growth and reach pupation.

To add insult to injury, the adult flies feed on the decomposing bodies of slugs and snails killed by the larvae.

Some firefly larvae are specialists, feeding exclusively on slugs and snails.

Centipedes

With their many scuttling legs, centipedes are an intimidating enemy and are able to attack large prey relative to their size. Their venomous jaws are actually modified front legs known as toxicognaths, which allow them to grab the prey and inject poison to paralyze it. Then their real jaws can get to work.

Centipedes in the *Lithobius* genus in the UK have the most records of slug-eating, along with other prey including spiders, fly larvae. earthworms, and springtails.

Friend
or foe?

HOW TO IDENTIFY SLUGS

Identifying which species of slug you're looking at is not always an easy task—both preparation and practice are needed.

Identification resources

Butterflies, bees, and birds have many enthusiasts and a plethora of books and apps available to help the beginner learn to identify them. No such abundance of resources exists for slugs. There are some free resources out there, such as the website of the Conchological Society and the USDA's Terrestrial Mollusk Tool (idtools.org/mollusk/).

The most thorough and reliable way to work toward identification is using the Field Studies Council's *Slugs of Britain and Ireland* book, which has a step-by-step guide and many high-quality photographs. This is the book that I have learned the most from, and it provides many of the slug statistics in the following pages.

Even armed with a book and training, slug identification is still hard going, as RHS student Imogen Cavadino found during her Slugs Count project. We recruited 60 gardeners from across the UK and provided video-call training, a slug-hunting kit, and feedback on their identifications while they completed a year's worth of monthly surveys. Their ID skills measurably improved over time, but they were

The size of a fully extended slug is one feature used to tell the difference between species.

still misidentifying one-third of their slugs by the end of the year. This difficulty meant that while 95 percent said they enjoyed taking part, only 66 percent said they were keen to continue recording slugs.

This chapter, therefore, won't be a one-stop shop for slug identification, but it will help you get a feel for it and recognize some of the most charismatic species.

Size matters

The size of a fully extended slug is one feature used to tell the difference between species, so it's worth having a ruler in your slug ID kit. However, a juvenile individual from a large species can send you on an ID wild-goose chase. This is particularly true where the young ones have stripes or other patterns that they lose by adulthood. You can sometimes spot a young one as having proportionally larger upper tentacles (cute!).

Sizing up slugs

The normal length of an extended slug ranges from a minimum (shown here in black) to a maximum (in gray). They can be much smaller when contracted (see p54).

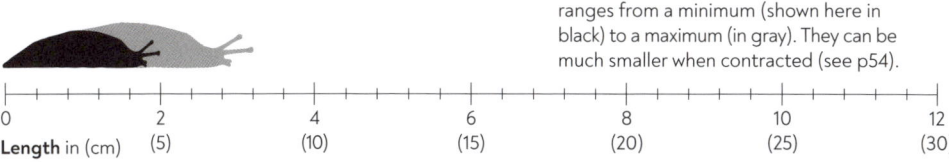

0	2	4	6	8	10	12

Length in (cm) (5) (10) (15) (20) (25) (30)

Touchy-feely

The key identification features are not only on all sides of the slug, but also include the color of the slime. Photos are often insufficient—you will need to pick up and handle the slug. A magnifying glass or hand lens will be helpful for some of the smaller or more subtle features.

Dabbing a piece of tissue or white paper on your new friend will help to make the slime color obvious. Sometimes, slightly more pressured dabbing is needed to get the slug to produce mucus.

Slug-handling safety

Slugs travel under- and overground, and many species feed on animal feces. Additionally, slugs and snails can transmit rat lungworm to humans, an unpleasant disease that is present in a number of tropical countries and the US, and which has also been detected in southern Europe. Consequently, you should always wash your hands with soap and water after handling slugs, and consider wearing disposable rubber gloves when handling them.

This doesn't mean you need to avoid handling them completely, however, as most cases of disease are traced back to someone eating a raw slug or snail. So please do get up close and personal with the slugs, but don't be tempted to taste them.

The key identification features are not only on all sides of the slug, but also include the color of the slime.

Slug body shapes
Most slugs you will encounter in the
garden have a similar body plan, with
a mantle on their back, but some
species are more unique.

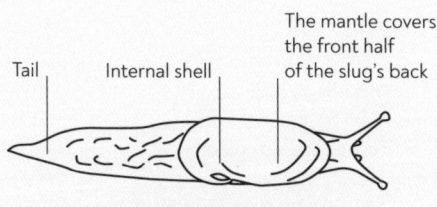

Tail | Internal shell | The mantle covers the front half of the slug's back

AGRIOLIMACID SLUG

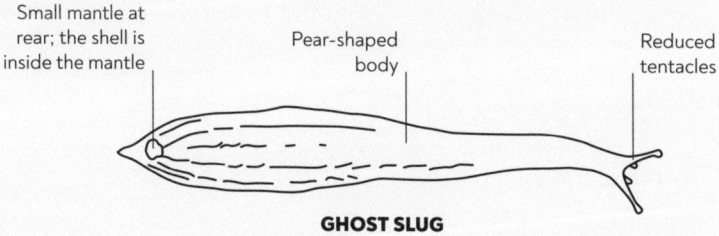

Small mantle at rear; the shell is inside the mantle | Pear-shaped body | Reduced tentacles

GHOST SLUG

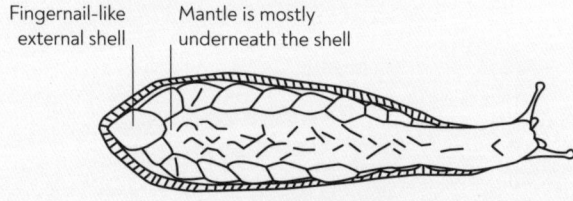

Fingernail-like external shell | Mantle is mostly underneath the shell

SHELLED SLUG

THE ANATOMY OF A SLUG

To get started with slug identification, you need to know which end is which. At the front end, you will find a head with a mouth and four tentacles.

Sensitive tentacles
The two tentacles on top have light-sensitive spots similar to eyes. The two smaller ones below are mostly used to smell/taste the ground. When resting or retreating from a threat, these may be completely withdrawn into the head.

The mantle, tail, and keel
The mantle looks like a saddle on the back starting just behind the head. Then the tail begins, usually taking up more than half of the slug's body length. The tail may have a keel, which is a ridge along the upper edge (imagine the keel of a boat if it were flipped upside down). This is an

Tail

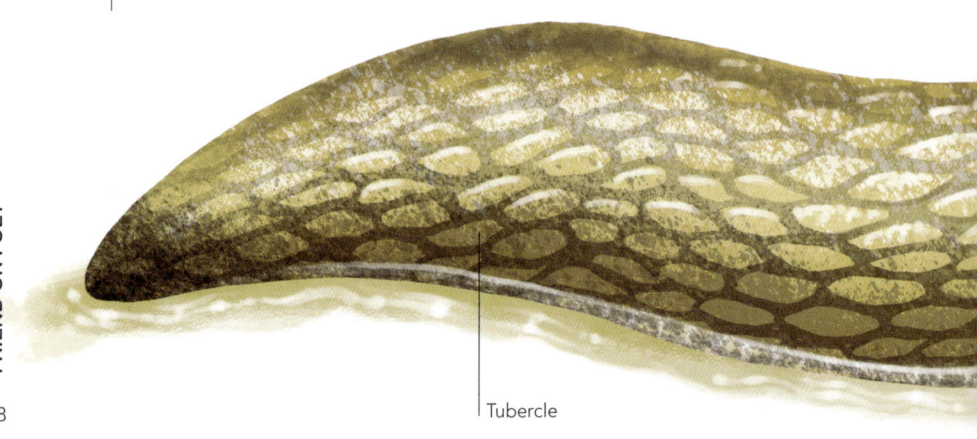

Tubercle

important feature for identification, so you might want to observe a range of slugs to learn to recognize it.

The sole

The whole underside of the slug is known as the sole, which makes sense for a gastropod, or "stomach foot" (see p14). This may or may not have a foot fringe, which is a band or frill between the sole and the main body.

Body orifices

Due to the slug's unique evolution from snails (see pp14–15), all the important bodily orifices can be found on the right-hand side of the mantle. The visible one, which is needed for identification purposes, is the breathing pore, or pneumostome. This may be mostly closed if the slug is resting or trying to conserve moisture.

Texture and tubercles

Texture is also a relevant feature for identification, including fine lines on the mantle and the tubercles of the body. Tubercles are the small ridges or lumps across the body, which are subtle in some types of slugs and very pronounced in others. Note that you won't see all these things when the slug is contracted (see p54).

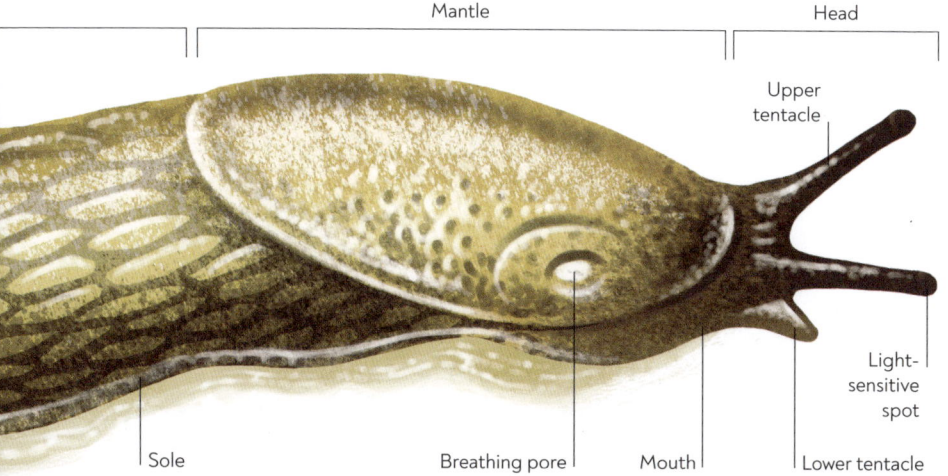

Mantle

Head

Upper tentacle

Light-sensitive spot

Sole

Breathing pore

Mouth

Lower tentacle

HAPPY FAMILIES

There are four main families of slugs in the UK (and potentially many more in the US and Canada). Learning to recognize these is a big step toward finding out who's who.

Arionidae—round-backed slugs

If you look at the right-hand side of an arionid slug, the mantle looks somewhat like a semicircle. Mentally draw a line vertically halfway through this semicircle to see whether the breathing pore is nearer the front or back. In the U.S. arionid slugs are the only introduced slugs to have their breathing pore in the front half of the mantle, but some native slugs in the family Ariolimacidae also have their breathing pore in the front half of the mantle.

They also have a mucus pore on the tip of the tail, which is sometimes obscured by a glob of mud or other debris. Many species have a prominent or colorful foot fringe. The mucus of these slugs tends toward the very sticky.

Adults from this group range from ¾ to 5½in (2 to 14cm) in length. Quite a few of the garden-plant munchers come from this group, although, on the whole, they are detritivores (they eat dead and rotting material) and omnivores (they eat a bit of everything).

Milacidae—long-keeled slugs

The milacids have their breathing pore in the back half of their mantle. Their name comes from the keel running the full length of their tail from mantle edge to tail tip. This tail tip has a blunt end instead of tapering gently.

Learning to recognize the four slug families is a big step toward finding out who's who.

Key identifying features
The key features of slugs from the
Arionidae and Milacidae families are
shown here.

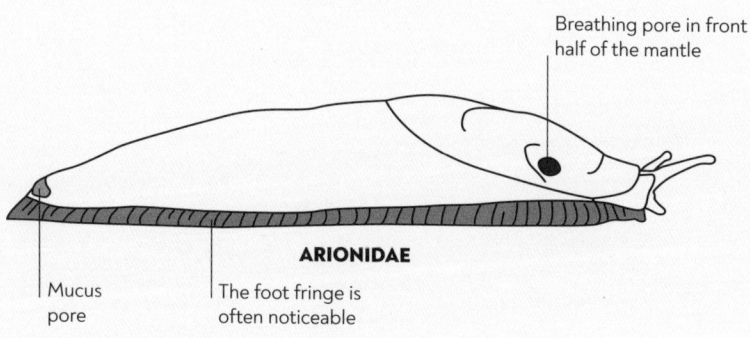

Breathing pore in front
half of the mantle

ARIONIDAE

Mucus
pore

The foot fringe is
often noticeable

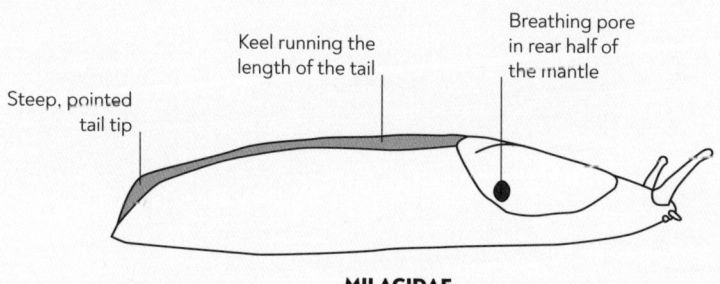

Keel running the
length of the tail

Breathing pore
in rear half of
the mantle

Steep, pointed
tail tip

MILACIDAE

Key identifying features
The key features of slugs from the
Limacidae and Agriolimacidae
families are shown here.

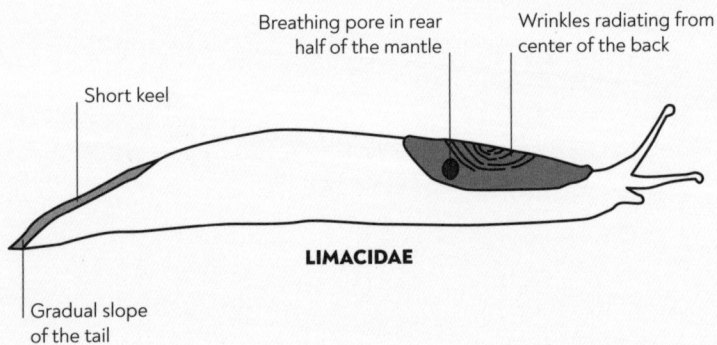

Breathing pore in rear
half of the mantle

Wrinkles radiating from
center of the back

Short keel

LIMACIDAE

Gradual slope
of the tail

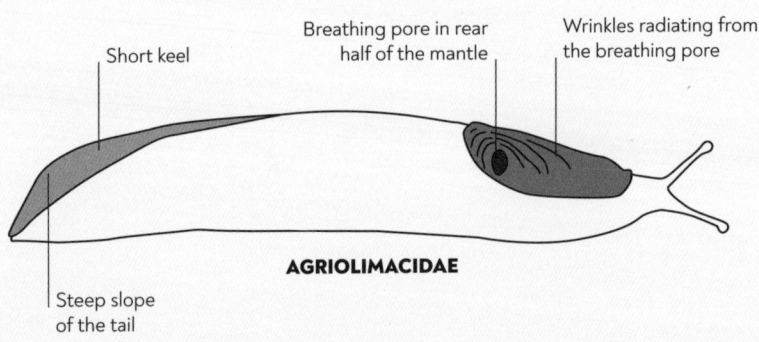

Breathing pore in rear
half of the mantle

Wrinkles radiating from
the breathing pore

Short keel

AGRIOLIMACIDAE

Steep slope
of the tail

The agriolimacids can be visually separated from the limacids by a steeper slope to the tail.

Adults from this family range from 1 to 3in (2.5 to 7.5cm), and they are often elusive, living mostly underground.

Limacidae—short-keeled slugs

The limacids also have their breathing pore in the back half of their mantle. They are so named because the keel reaches only partway up their back from the tail tip, which has a gradual taper. This family has a very fine pattern of ridges radiating out from the center of the mantle on the back.

The limacids contain some of the largest species, with adults ranging from 1⅜ to 8in (3.5 to 20cm) in length. Slugs in this group are mostly friends, specializing in eating fungi, algae, and other detritus, but a few are omnivorous, so they might occasionally nibble your plants.

Agriolimacidae—short-keeled slugs

The agriolimacids can be visually separated from the limacids by a steeper slope to the tail, and the ridges on the mantle radiate around the breathing pore. For both the short-keeled families, it might take a while to spot the keel because it often blends in with the body in color—which is why it's important to look across all features of the mantle and tail to identify the correct family.

Much smaller than the limacids, they are only ⅝ to 2in (1.5 to 5cm) when fully grown. But the small size of the agriolimacids belies their munching power: some of the most herbivorous species sit in this family. Globally, they have the highest number of slug species of any slug family and are the most widely spread.

GETTING ACQUAINTED

It's time to get to know some of the most common garden slugs, and a few rarer and more exciting ones. The profiles are grouped by family (see pp50–53), and each profile has a quick facts list.

 Common name
First things first when getting acquainted.

 Scientific name The scientific name is very important because different versions of common names might be used in different places. It consists of two words, the first being the genus and the second the specific, or species, name. Closely related species have the same genus, but the species name is a unique and universal identifier.

 Family Families are another way that scientists group related organisms—the family level groups several genera that are closely related. Members of a slug family all share some key features of identification, so the family name is essential for identification because of all the key features it implies. These are shown on pp51 and 52. Some might also have a subfamily name because scientists absolutely love labeling and organizing the natural world.

 Size This refers to the length of a fully grown adult, measured when stretched out as if crawling along. An alarmed slug will contract itself to a much shorter length, so you might need to sit and watch before it stretches out again. Each slug profiled shows the proportionate length in a range from usual minimum (shown in black) to maximum (shown in gray), but it's not to scale.

Found Information on what kind of habitats you can see them. All of the slugs featured are native to or found in the UK and northwest Europe, but most are also established in the US and other places in the world.

Eats What their preferred foodstuff is, or if they are an omnivore (eat everything).

Identification Given that slugs are generally tricky to identify, this is a slightly haphazard scale that ranges from easy and medium difficulty to difficult and complicated.

Friend or foe?

For each profile, we'll look at whether the slug is a friend or foe, or neutral. Of the 45 well-known slug species in Britain and Ireland, only seven are considered significant pests, eating enough plant matter to cause a problem for farmers and gardeners.

Seventeen are worthy of the "friend" tag, helping to recycle dead material or occupying another ecosystem niche that doesn't clash with humans.

Another 11 are neutral. This group contains mostly omnivorous species, which sometimes eat dead material and other times live plants.

Finally, 10 species are still unknown. These are species that are fairly new to the UK, or that are so rare and elusive that scientists aren't sure of their diet.

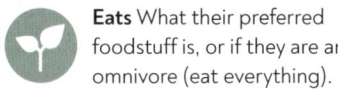

- Friend
- Foe
- Neutral
- Unknown

Who's who?

Of the 45 slug species in Britain and Ireland, 7 are considered pests, 11 are neutral, 17 are friends, and 10 are unknown. Of the 87 US species, 64 are assumed friends and 23 are possible foes.

LARGE BLACK & RED SLUGS

Scientific name
Arion ater and *Arion rufus*

Family Arionidae

Size 2½–5½in (6–14cm)

Found Everywhere

Eats Omnivorous

Identification Complicated

Color variations

The common names of these two species, large black slug and large red slug, refer to their most stereotypical color forms, but both occur in many shades of beige, gray, and brown. The large red often has a contrasting orange foot fringe and orangey tones on its sole. A rather pushy way to tell the difference is to repeatedly prod the slug until it contracts fully, whereupon the large black slug should rock noticeably from side to side. This is entertaining, but the large red can do it too to some extent, and I've not found it to be a straightforward method to confirm. To add further to the confusion, it increasingly seems that these two species can hybridize with each other and with the invasive vulgar slug (see p58).

They can only reliably be distinguished by dissecting specimens to examine features of the genitalia. While this is a worthwhile activity to produce accurate records of slug biodiversity, it is probably something that you and your new slug acquaintances are disinclined to get involved with.

Friend or foe?

The large size of these slugs means they can be active in drier conditions than many other slugs, so are often seen roaming about in daylight. This visibility means they often get blamed for holes in plants, but smaller, more secretive slugs may be the true culprits.

The large *Arion* slugs are highly omnivorous, and will eat dead leaves, dead slugs, other dead animals, poop, cat and dog food, seedlings, and other soft, live plant material. They are allies for their recycling/tidying abilities, but their large size means they can also make short work of a row of seedlings in springtime.

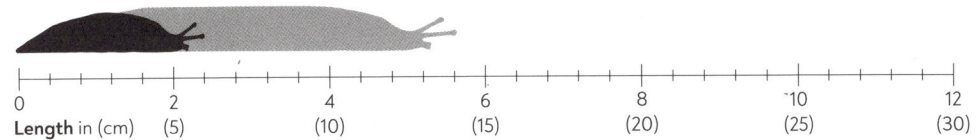

Length in (cm) 0 2 (5) 4 (10) 6 (15) 8 (20) 10 (25) 12 (30)

LARGE BLACK SLUG
The sole can be dark but paler than the body. The slug will usually rock from side to side when prodded.

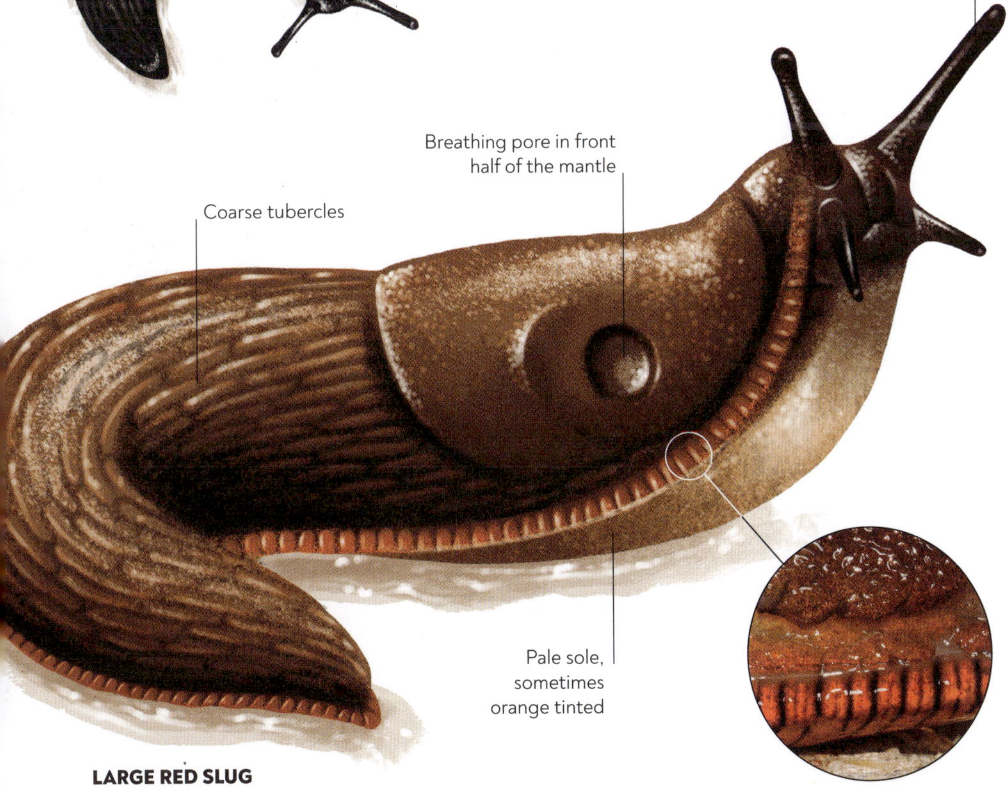

Dark tentacles

Coarse tubercles

Breathing pore in front half of the mantle

Pale sole, sometimes orange tinted

LARGE RED SLUG

Foot fringe
Often bright orange and always with stripes.

VULGAR SLUG

Scientific name *Arion vulgaris*

Family Arionidae

Size 2½–5½in (6–14cm)

Found Not established in US; farmland and gardens

Eats Plants and more

Identification Complicated

Color variations

People in the UK may know the vulgar slug by the common name Spanish slug, as it has featured in the press due to being an invasive species. However, that name is inaccurate as scientists now think Spain is where it first started invading rather than its source, which may be somewhere in Central Europe. Regardless of its origin, it has been spreading and damaging crops and native fauna in the UK and mainland Europe, and is now classed as one of the most invasive species in Europe.

Its appearance is similar to red-brown forms of the large black and large red slug (see p56), but can often be distinguished from them by a dark rim around the breathing pore and a dark-colored sole. These three, but especially the vulgar slug and the large red, can probably hybridize, making these diagnostic features likely to get muddier over time.

Friend or foe?

Non-native species are often more problematic than similar native ones, and this is definitely true for the vulgar slug, which has been gradually establishing and becoming a problem for farmers across Europe for decades. However, in the UK, there's some evidence it is not quite as impactful as in mainland Europe. It has a big appetite and often occurs in high numbers, so it definitely falls on the "foe" end of the scale.

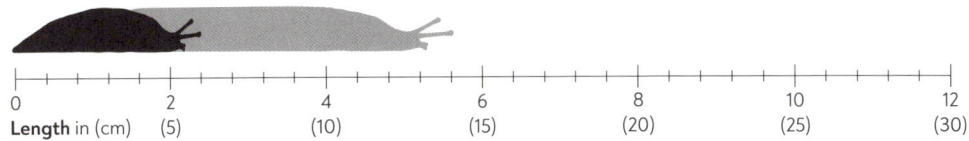

Length in (cm) 0 2 (5) 4 (10) 6 (15) 8 (20) 10 (25) 12 (30)

The vulgar slug does not rock from side to side when prodded, unlike the large black slug.

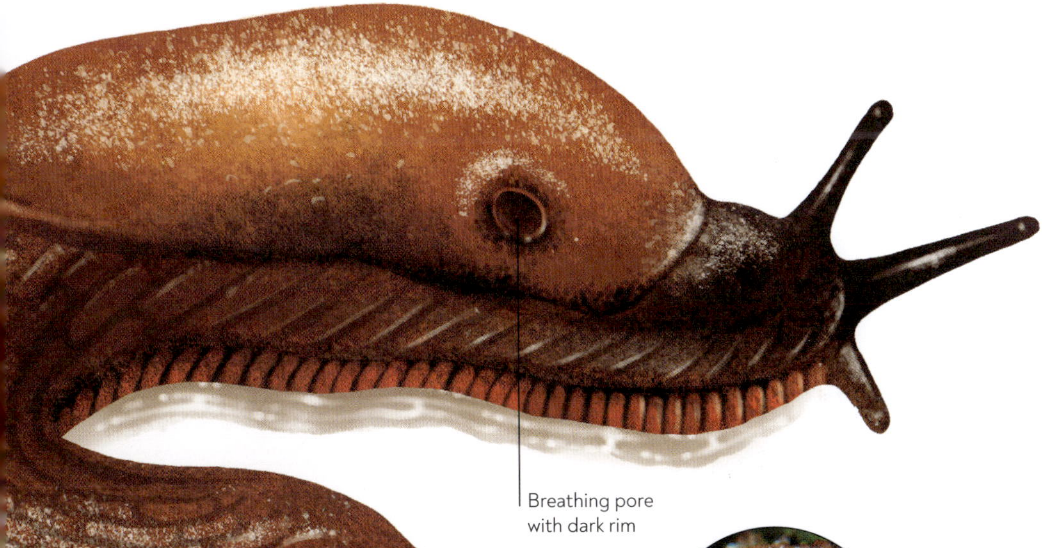

Breathing pore
with dark rim

Dark orange striped
foot fringe

Dark sole
The sole is dark
gray in color.

GREEN-SOLED SLUG

Scientific name
Arion flagellus

Family Arionidae

Size 2½–4in (6–10cm)

Found Not found in the US; disturbed habitats in Europe

Eats Not known

Identification Medium difficulty

Color variations

Our last profile from the large *Arion* group, the green-soled slug is noticeable for its very coarse tubercles (the lumpy texture on the skin of the tail). The other key feature is its namesake, a pale green-tinged sole. It also has the common name Durham slug, after the English city where it was first described, but unlike the vulgar (Spanish) slug (see p58), this species probably is native to the Iberian peninsula.

Friend or foe?

The green-soled slug is one of several slug species found in the UK for which we simply don't have enough information about their biology and ecology to know whether they are a problem or not. It's not even been definitively confirmed when they first appeared in Britain and Ireland. *Slugs of Britain and Ireland* mentions them reaching high numbers in gardens, and we also found this in the Slugs Count project (see pp44–45). So we don't know whether they are eating plants or sticking mostly to dead stuff, and they definitely merit further study.

Tubercles
Coarsest tubercles of all the large *Arion* slugs.

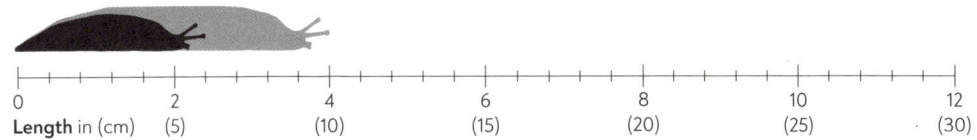

Length in (cm) 0 2 (5) 4 (10) 6 (15) 8 (20) 10 (25) 12 (30)

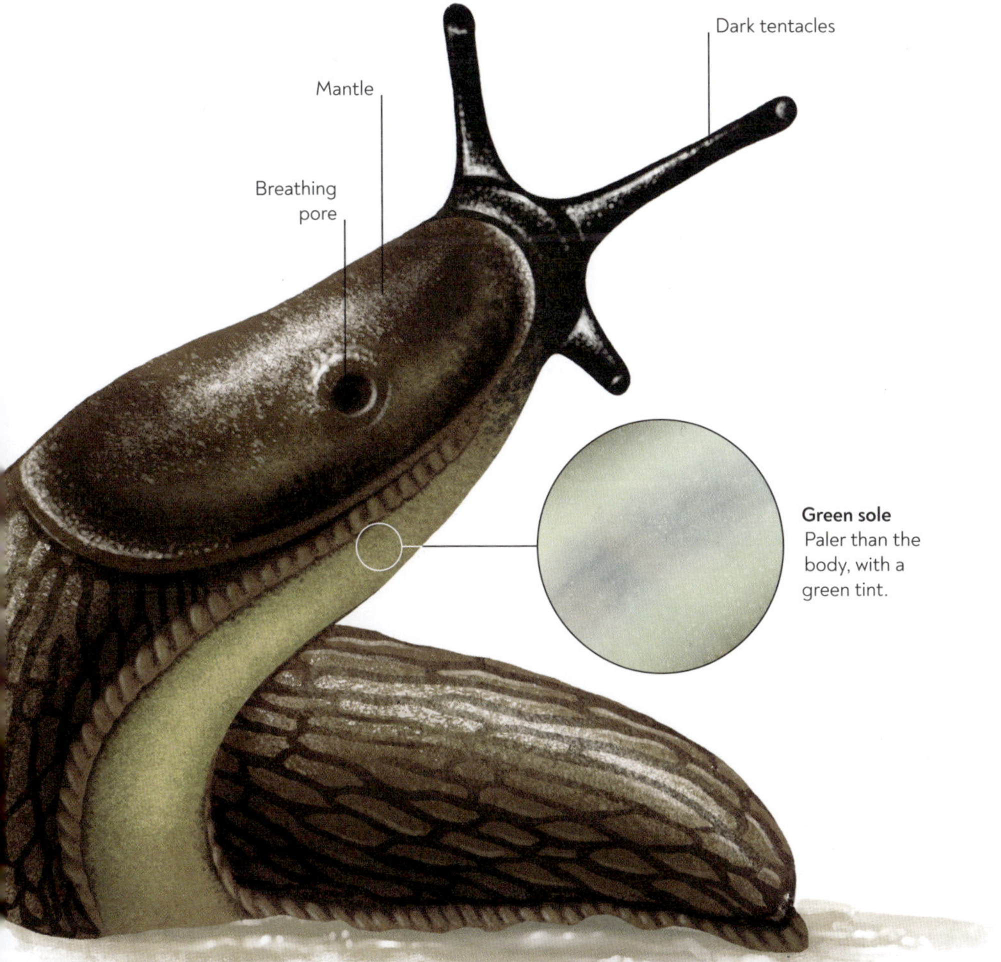

Mantle

Dark tentacles

Breathing pore

Green sole
Paler than the body, with a green tint.

DUSKY SLUG

Scientific name
Arion subfuscus

Family Arionidae (*Mesarion*)

Size 2–2¾in (5–7cm)

Found Everywhere

Eats Omnivorous

Identification
Medium difficulty–difficult

Color variations

A medium-sized slug, often with a stripe high up along each side, the dusky slug's most recognizable features are orange mucus and a pale whitish-gray sole. It belongs to the *Mesarion* subgenus of the *Arion* genus, which contains two other species that are hard to distinguish but are much more rare.

For the beginner slug identifier, it's going to be particularly hard to tell the difference between this species and juveniles of the large *Arion* species, as they're all somewhat striped, but the dusky slug has less coarse tubercles.

Friend or foe?
Another very omnivorous *Arion*, this one isn't considered a significant problem in the UK. It probably eats lots of rotting plant material, but has been known to eat garden plants, too. It is, however,

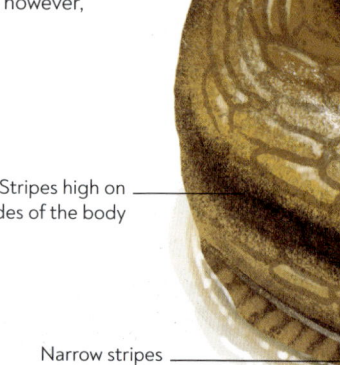

Stripes high on sides of the body

Narrow stripes on foot fringe

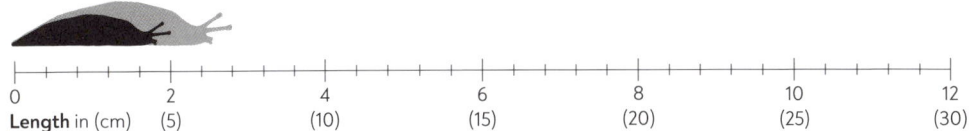

Length in (cm)

| 0 | 2 (5) | 4 (10) | 6 (15) | 8 (20) | 10 (25) | 12 (30) |

non-native and increasingly widespread in North America, as are some of the other *Arion* species.

As with the vulgar slug (see p58) in Europe, species can sometimes be annoyingly successful when removed from their native range into a new place. This may be due to the absence of natural predators and parasites, something known in ecological science as the enemy-release hypothesis.

The dusky slug probably eats lots of rotting plant material, but has been known to eat garden plants, too.

Orange mucus may give an orange tint to the body

BROWN & BLUE-BLACK SOIL SLUGS

Scientific name
Arion distinctus and
Arion hortensis

Family Arionidae (*Kobeltia*)

Size ¾–1½in (2–4cm)

Found Widespread and
common in gardens

Eats Plants

Identification Difficult

Color variations

These two species are the most commonly found members of a subgenus of slugs (the *Kobeltia*) that all have orangey mucus and an orangey sole. Their small size and subtle differences in features mean that a beginner is not likely to identify them easily, even if they have an ID guide in front of them. Both have stripes low down on their sides. The common names are the clue to their difference – one has more brown colourations and the other more blue – but the Slugs Count project (see pp44–45) didn't find this to be a reliable feature when identifying slugs. Here, as with the large *Arion* species, expert examination and/or dissection would be needed to confirm identity.

Friend or foe?
The soil slugs feed on roots and shoots, causing problems in farms and gardens. They are some of the most notable pestiferous slugs in both their European home range and in many countries where they are introduced, especially North America.

Length in (cm)

| 0 | 2 (5) | 4 (10) | 6 (15) | 8 (20) | 10 (25) | 12 (30) |

Brown-black tentacles

BLUE-BLACK SOIL SLUG

Orangey sole
Colored by orangey mucus.

Stripe low down on side of the body

Stripe low down on the side, often with contrasting white stripe before the foot fringe

BROWN SOIL SLUG

Blue-black tentacles

TAWNY SOIL SLUG

Scientific name *Arion owenii*

Family Arionidae (*Kobeltia*)

Size 1–1½in (2.5–4cm)

Found Not found in the US; wetter regions in Europe

Eats Not known

Identification Medium difficulty

Color variations

Compared to the other soil slugs, the tawny soil slug has a distinct tawny color with stylish dark stripes along its side and more diffusely down the middle of its back. It does not seem to be spread as widely as the other soil slugs and is mostly found in wet, wild habitats, but is sometimes seen in more urban areas. It was first described in County Donegal, Ireland, and most records of it are concentrated in a few areas of Ireland and Britain, with just a handful of reports from elsewhere in Europe.

Friend or foe?
The tawny soil slug is infrequently seen to be a problem, but, as a result, we also don't know what its preferred foodstuffs are. It has been reported being spread in horticultural waste for some time, but as this doesn't seem to be linked to any activity in gardens, it's not likely to be a reason for concern.

The tawny soil slug is mostly found in wet, wild habitats but is sometimes seen in more urban areas.

Length in (cm)

0   2 (5)   4 (10)   6 (15)   8 (20)   10 (25)   12 (30)

Diffuse stripe on side of the body

Yellowy-orange mucus

Tubercles are fairly coarse or "warty"

Dark tentacles

HEDGEHOG SLUG

Scientific name
Arion intermedius

Family: Arionidae (*Kobeltia*)

Size ⅝–¾in (1.5–2cm)

Found Everywhere

Eats Mostly dead plant material and fungi

Identification Easy

Color variations

If you could be convinced that slugs can be cute, this is the one to do it! The hedgehog slug is named for its prickly appearance when contracted or in dry or cold conditions. The "prickles" are its tubercles, contracted into a pointy shape. It is also the tiniest of the *Arion* slugs.

This slug is one of the species that can reproduce by fertilizing itself (very efficient). It used to be thought that the hedgehog slug reproduced almost entirely by self-fertilization, but more recent studies show that it can and does reproduce by mating.

Friend or foe?
This is another species that has been exported worldwide, but it is not as bothersome as its cousins. It does seem to prefer rotting material and fungi, and can probably be excused a little leaf nibbling for its adorable appearance.

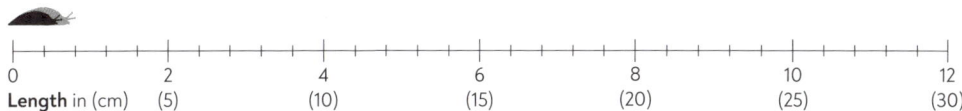

Length in (cm) | 0 | 2 (5) | 4 (10) | 6 (15) | 8 (20) | 10 (25) | 12 (30)

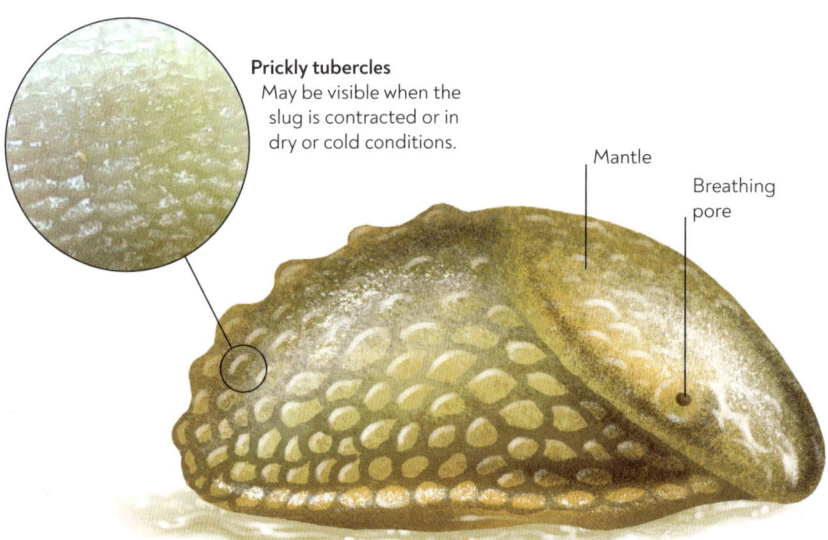

Prickly tubercles
May be visible when the slug is contracted or in dry or cold conditions.

Mantle

Breathing pore

CONTRACTED POSE

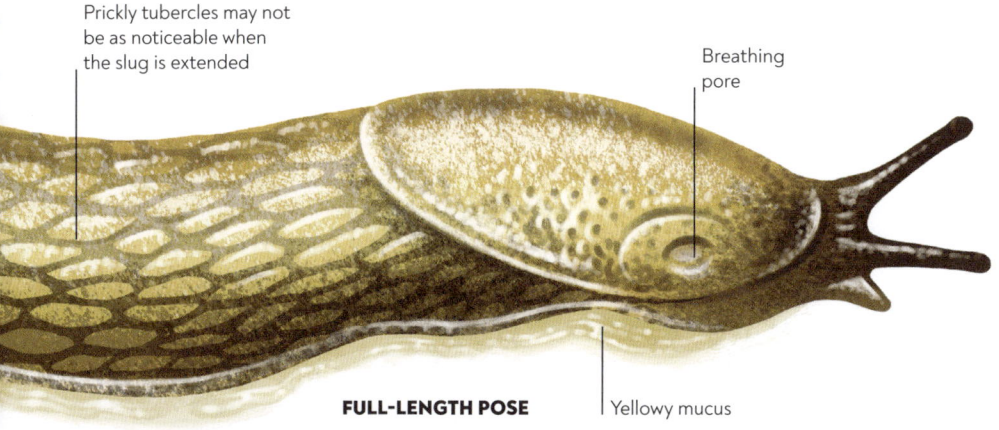

Prickly tubercles may not be as noticeable when the slug is extended

Breathing pore

FULL-LENGTH POSE

Yellowy mucus

KERRY SLUG

Scientific name
Geomalacus maculosus

Family Arionidae

Size 2½–3½in (6–9cm)

Found Not found in the US; scrub and bog in Europe

Eats Lichen, fungi, and algae

Identification Easy

Color variations

This is an extremely special slug. It is very distinctive, covered in pale spots against a darker background. It tucks itself up into a ball when alarmed by folding its foot in half.

The Kerry slug lives in scrub, heath, and bog, which might explain why its foodstuffs are damp-loving fungi and plantlike organisms.

Friend or foe?
A friend in need! This is the only legally protected slug species in Europe and possibly the world, making it onto the International Union for Conservation of Nature (IUCN) Red List. Its global presence is limited to west and southwest Ireland and northwest Portugal and Spain. Fortunately, it seems to be doing well in Ireland, where there are lots of protection efforts in place.

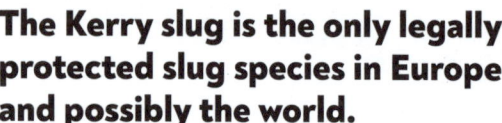

The Kerry slug is the only legally protected slug species in Europe and possibly the world.

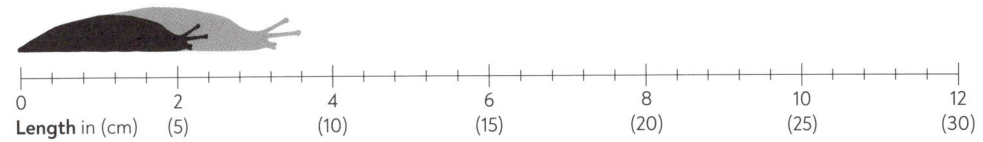

Length in (cm)   0   2 (5)   4 (10)   6 (15)   8 (20)   10 (25)   12 (30)

Alarmed pose
It can fold its foot in half to roll into a ball when alarmed.

Pale spots on a gray-brown background

Pale sole

Foot fringe slightly paler than the body

BUDAPEST KEELED SLUG

Scientific name
Tandonia budapestensis

Family Milacidae

Size 2–2¾in (5–7cm)

Found Limited distribution in the US; underground

Eats Roots and tubers

Identification
Medium difficulty

Color variations

The Budapest keeled slug can be distinguished from the other *Tandonia* long-keeled slugs by the pattern on its sole, which is pale with a dark, diffuse stripe down the middle. It also often rests in a C-shape.

The other *Tandonia* species look quite similar, but most are much rarer, and, in fact, it is the most common of the milacid slugs worldwide. Only the Sowerby's keeled slug, *T. sowerbyi*, comes close, but Sowerby's is more yellow in color and has yellow mucus.

Friend or foe?
This is the most likely culprit for the holes in your potatoes. Their mostly underground life means they can munch away hidden from view, and you don't notice the holey potatoes until it comes to harvest time. They break the skin of potatoes, which can allow other creatures and rot in, which is very frustrating. There's also evidence that they are toxic to ground beetles, one of our best slug predators (see pp40, 125). However, they are susceptible to the nematode parasite, which can be used as a biological control (see p130), so all is not lost.

The Budapest keeled slug is susceptible to the nematode parasite, which can be used as a biological control.

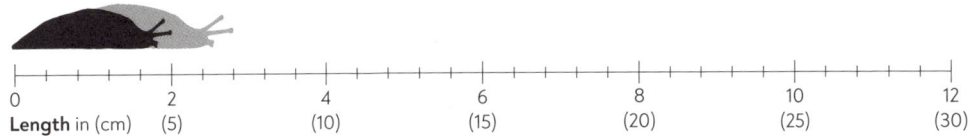

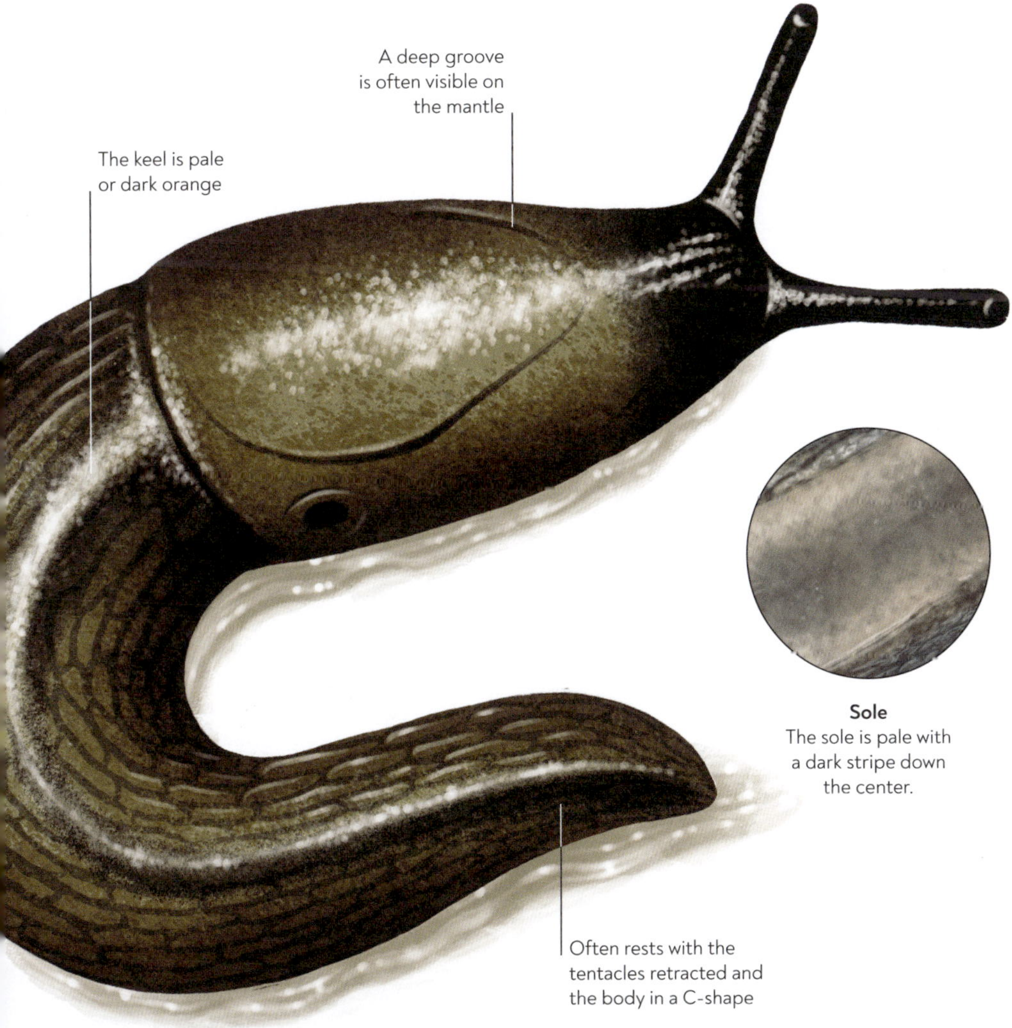

Length in (cm)
0 2 (5) 4 (10) 6 (15) 8 (20) 10 (25) 12 (30)

A deep groove is often visible on the mantle

The keel is pale or dark orange

Sole
The sole is pale with a dark stripe down the center.

Often rests with the tentacles retracted and the body in a C-shape

SMOOTH JET SLUG

Scientific name
Milax gagates

Family Milacidae

Size 1¾–2¼in (4.5–5.5cm)

Found Warmer, wet areas

Eats Roots, tubers, and more

Identification
Medium difficulty

Color variations

Another descriptive common name; this slug has a smoother or silkier texture than the *Tandonia* slugs. It has a less obvious keel because it is the same color as the body, but when it is contracted, its keel sticks up much more noticeably. Another diagnostic feature is a dark outline around the breathing pore.

This species also has the common name greenhouse slug, and although it can be found outside, it does seem to need slightly warmer temperatures to thrive. This inclination or tolerance for warmth may explain why it has established widely around the world (as long as there's enough rain).

Friend or foe?
Like the Budapest keeled slug (see p72), the smooth jet slug can cause problems for gardeners by feeding on the underground parts of plants. This is the most common species of millacid slug in the US, and farmers in other parts of the world, such as South America, have had their crops severely damaged by it.

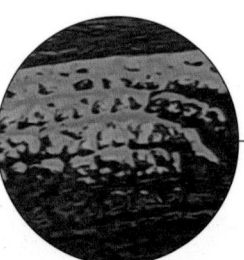

Keel
The keel is usually the same color as the body, or slightly darker.

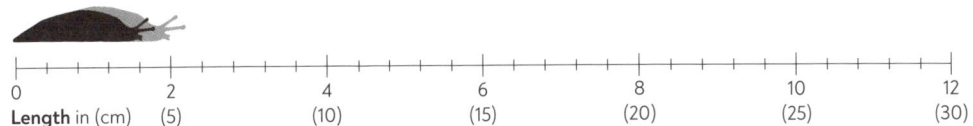

Length in (cm)

| 0 | 2 (5) | 4 (10) | 6 (15) | 8 (20) | 10 (25) | 12 (30) |

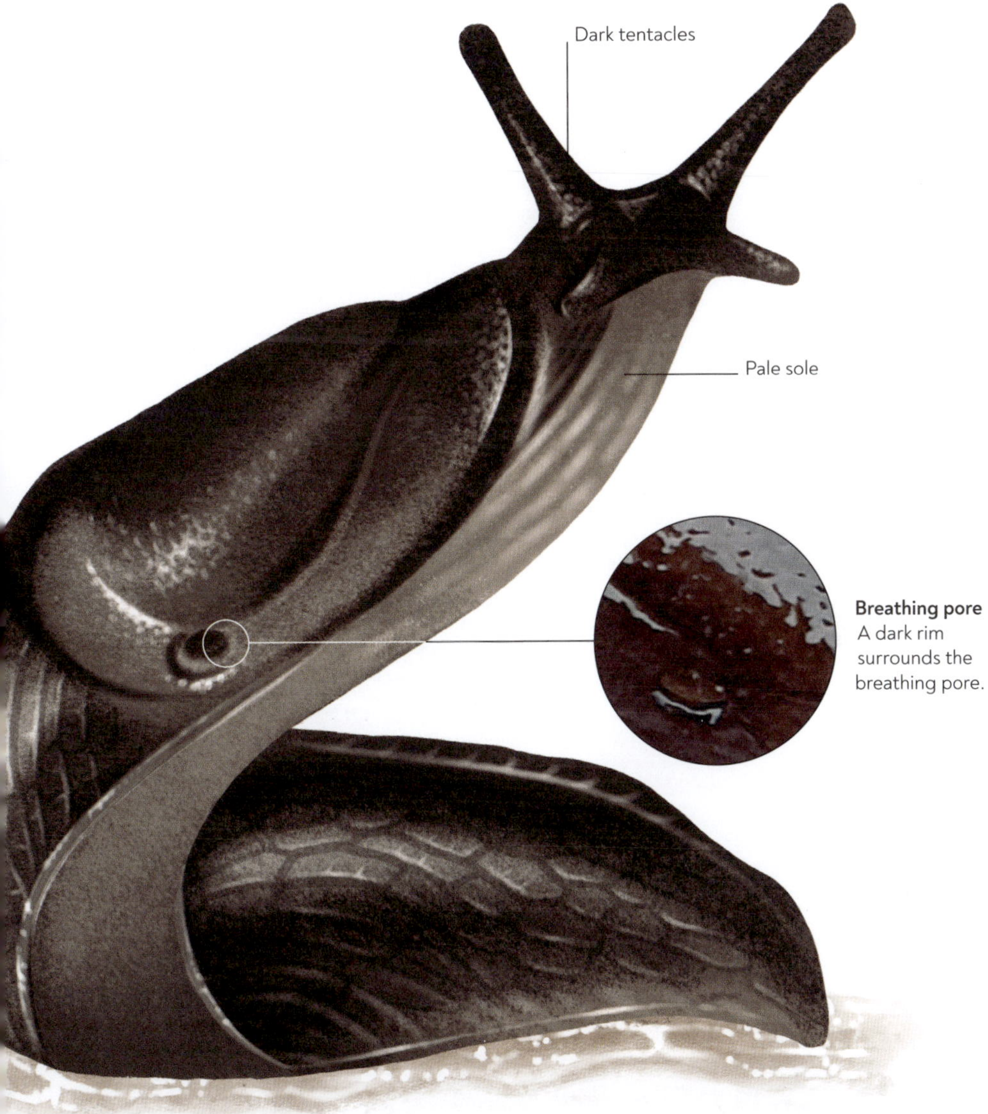

Dark tentacles

Pale sole

Breathing pore
A dark rim
surrounds the
breathing pore.

LEOPARD SLUG

Scientific name
Limax maximus

Family Limacidae

Size 4–6in (10–15cm)

Found Common in forests, scrub, and gardens

Eats Omnivorous

Identification Easy

Color variations

The leopard slug is one of the best-known species of slug thanks to its spotty appearance and spectacular mating behavior. The courting couple climbs up a tree and onto a branch to descend on a rope of slime. They twirl gracefully around each other and mate in mid-air. Once this process is completed, they either climb back up the rope or sever it and drop unceremoniously to the ground to go their separate ways. A rather long-lived slug, this species can live up to three years, so there are lots of opportunities for acrobatic mating.

Leopard slugs are often very easy to identify due to their large size and striking dark spots that give them their name. Very lightly spotted or overall dark individuals can cause confusion, though.

Friend or foe?

Leopard slugs eat fungi, lichen, dead plant material, and occasionally live plant material too. On balance, they are a gardener's friend, however, due to their territorial nature. They are often cited as eating other slugs, but it's more likely that they are just attacking (sometimes lethally) because of their territoriality rather than for food.

Length in (cm)

0   2   4   6   8   10   12
    (5)   (10)   (15)   (20)   (25)   (30)

Short keel

Leopard slugs mating
These slugs create an
acrobatic display as they
descend on a rope of slime
to mate in mid-air.

Leopard pattern
The base color is beige-gray
with varying numbers
of dark spots.

Pale sole

Red-brown
tentacles

Slug genitalia
are bright white

ASH-BLACK SLUG

Scientific name
Limax cinereoniger

Family Limacidae

Size 4–6in (10–15cm)*

Found Not in the US; woodlands

Eats Mostly fungi

Identification Easy

Color variations

This species is a long, dark slug with a pale keel running about halfway up its back and a very distinct pale stripe in the center of the sole. It's superficially similar to the large black slug (see p56) if you are a slug ID beginner, which is why it's important to identify the family a slug belongs to first. It occasionally has spots or stripes, but only on the tail. It is one of our more long-lived slugs, and an individual can live more than five years.

Friend or foe?
The ash-black slug is "a slug of wild places," a woodland specialist, so it is not likely to interact with gardeners much. As an indicator of old or ancient forests, it can be considered a friend in the name of protecting biodiversity.

*The ash-black slug holds the record for the longest UK slug, with individuals up to 12in (30cm) long, but its usual length is more modest.

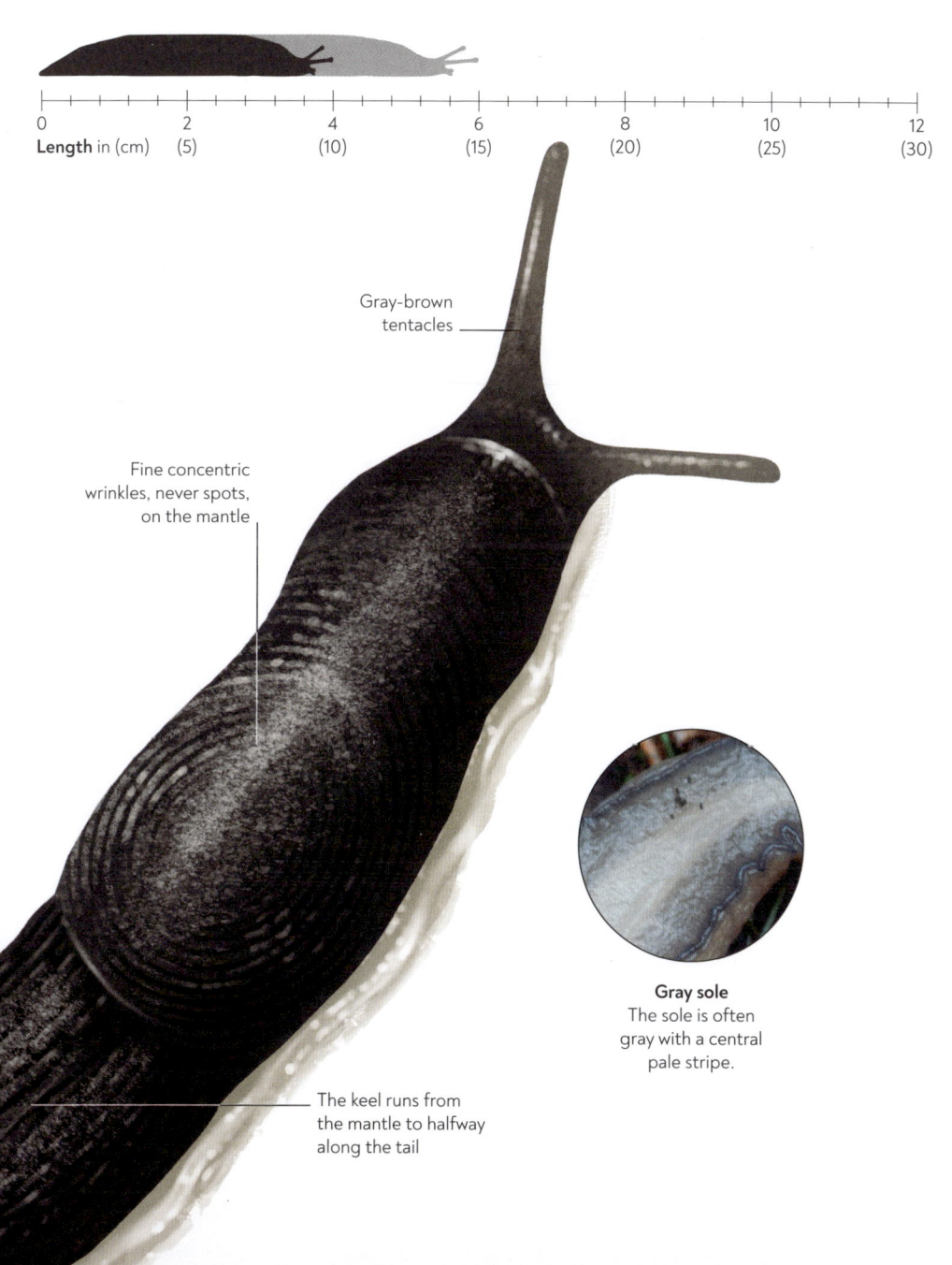

Length in (cm)
| 0 | 2 (5) | 4 (10) | 6 (15) | 8 (20) | 10 (25) | 12 (30) |

Gray-brown
tentacles

Fine concentric
wrinkles, never spots,
on the mantle

Gray sole
The sole is often
gray with a central
pale stripe.

The keel runs from
the mantle to halfway
along the tail

YELLOW CELLAR SLUG

Scientific name
Limacus flavus

Family Limacidae

Size 3–5in (8–13cm)

Found Near human habitation in gardens and urban areas

Eats Mold and algae

Identification Easy

Color variations

Despite the name, both the yellow cellar slug and the green cellar slug (see p82) come in various shades of yellow and green. Both have blue-gray tentacles and a mottled body pattern. The way to distinguish them is the pale stripe down the middle of the back, which goes the length of the body in the yellow cellar slug, and is not present or very short in the green.

We don't know for sure when the yellow cellar slug arrived in the UK, possibly from Mediterranean areas, but the first record in literature is 1685. It has always been associated with human habitation, and probably got its name from a time when houses weren't so thoroughly sealed and heated as they are today, and cellars were a common place to see them (with plenty of their food). They used to be common in the UK, but seem to be disappearing concurrently with the spread of the green cellar slug in the UK.

Friend or foe?
Despite being non-native, these slugs can be considered a friend because, from a human perspective, they are neutral or even beneficial if you count their cleaning and recycling of mold. Although there are many high-profile examples of invasive species causing havoc when moved around the world, in most cases, new arrivals actually slot into an ecosystem without catastrophic effects, especially if the move isn't far away.

The yellow cellar slug has always been associated with human habitation.

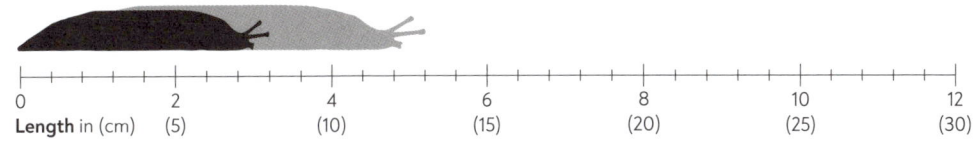

Length in (cm)

| 0 | 2 (5) | 4 (10) | 6 (15) | 8 (20) | 10 (25) | 12 (30) |

Pale stripe
along the tail

Fine tubercles

Blue-gray tentacles

Yellow or pale green
body with paler
splotches

GREEN CELLAR SLUG

Scientific name
Limacus maculatus

Family Limacidae

Size 3–5in (8–13cm)

Found Not found in the US; near human habitation in Europe

Eats Mold and algae

Identification Easy

Color variations

The green cellar slug is sometimes greener and always less striped than its close cousin, the yellow cellar slug (see p80). It was first recorded in Britain and Ireland in the 1970s, but at that time, it wasn't clear whether it had always been there and had been confused with the yellow cellar slug. The latest consensus is that it was a much later arrival, probably from the Caucasus and Crimea region, which has become widely established since the 1980s. The yellow has been decreasing, but it's not clear if that is a true decline, improved identification as the green, or because they can hybridize and offspring more closely resemble the green.

Perhaps a touch more omnivorous than the yellow, this slug has been noted eating wallpaper and pet food. The green cellar slug is particularly sociable, and these slugs are known to seek each other's company and that of the yellow cellar slug, sharing the same daytime hiding places and "huddling" in groups. Rather than this being a social behaviour, though, it is probably to help conserve water. These slug huddles can often be found on compost bin lids and under plant pots.

Friend or foe?
The green cellar slug is beneficial to humans based on its food choices, but possibly negative from a biodiversity viewpoint if it does turn out to be causing the decline of the yellow cellar slug. If it's just hybridizing with the yellow cellar slug, then it is neutral.

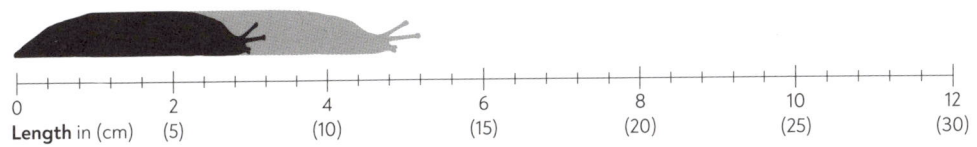

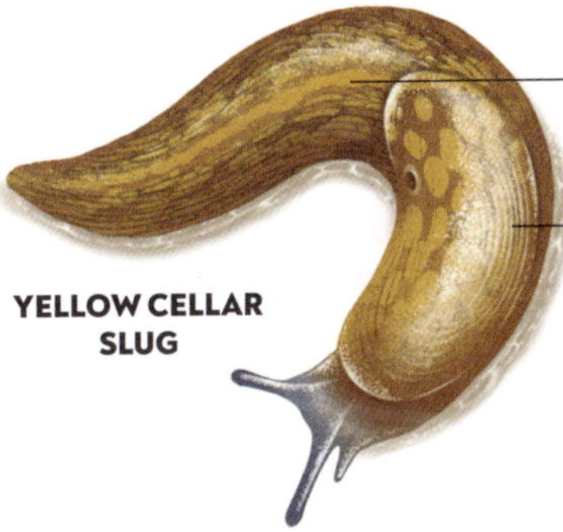

Length in (cm)   0   2   4   6   8   10   12
                      (5) (10) (15) (20) (25) (30)

YELLOW CELLAR SLUG

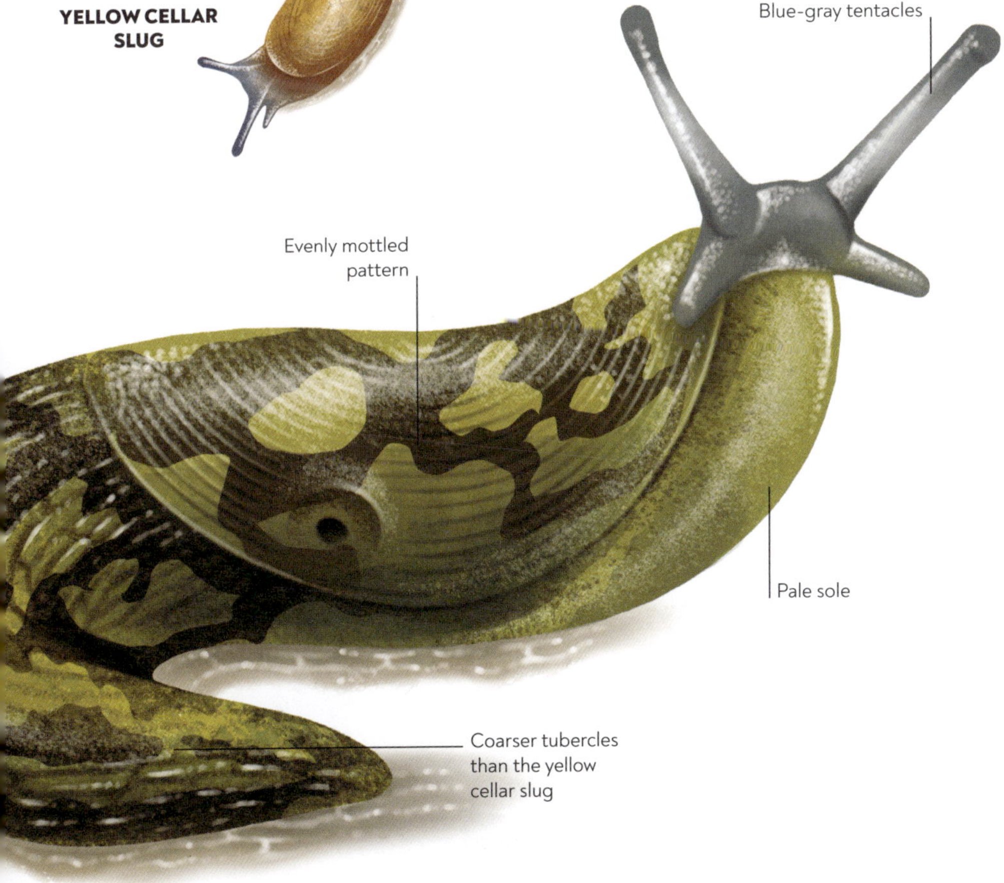

Pale stripe on the tail

Finer tubercles than the green cellar slug

Blue-gray tentacles

Evenly mottled pattern

Pale sole

Coarser tubercles than the yellow cellar slug

TREE SLUG

Scientific name
Lehmannia marginata

Family Limacidae

Size 2½–3½in (6–9cm)

Found Reports of US sightings

Eats Lichen, fungi, and algae

Identification
Medium difficulty

Color variations

The tree slug is pale and translucent, with stripes on the mantle that may be broken. It is similar to the threeband slugs (see p86) but more greeny-gray and with a pale stripe on the keel and on the back. They don't overlap much in habitat because this species occurs mostly in woods and on rocky hillsides.

They are named for climbing trees! They rest underground during the day, like most slugs, but then as night falls, they climb way up into the tree canopy to find their preferred food. When they set off, they are plump, translucent, and glistening, but by the time they descend, they have lost so much of their moisture that they are not nearly so elegant. They then hurry down to hide away before the sun rises.

Friend or foe?

Its diet and habitat mean that the tree slug doesn't interact much with humans, so can be considered a friend or neutral. This is my favorite slug because of a formative experience on a field identification course, learning from the charismatic slug expert Chris du Feu. The sight of their elegant forms on tree trunks really captivated me and propelled me along my path of fascination with slugs.

As its name suggests, the tree slug climbs high into the tree canopy to find its preferred food.

Length in (cm)

0	2	4	6
	(5)	(10)	(15)

Tree grazer
The tree slug climbs into the
canopy to graze on lichen,
fungi, and algae, and then
descends before dawn.

Diffuse, dark
bands along side
of the mantle

Translucent skin
The tree slug has shiny,
translucent skin, especially
when it is well hydrated.

Faint pale stripe along
center of the tail

THREEBAND SLUGS

Scientific name
Ambigolimax valentianus
and Ambigolimax
nyctelius

Family Limacidae

Size 2–3in (5–8cm)

Found Gardens

Eats Omnivorous

Identification Difficult

Color variations

More pinkish in coloration than the tree slug (see p84), these slugs have their namesake three stripes along the mantle and body, although the stripes can sometimes be very faint, especially the central one. The two species look quite different in the main photos in *Slugs of Britain and Ireland*, with *Ambigolimax nyctelius* much more strongly striped. However, the book does say they need to be dissected to separate with confidence (*A. valentianus* has an extra appendage on its penis).

In practice as a gardener and slug hobbyist, though, there's not much point in trying to distinguish between them. These slugs have also been through several taxonomic revisions (scientists renaming things), which is ongoing.

Friend or foe?
Non-natives that appeared in the UK from southwest and southeast Europe in the 1930s, and that were originally found in greenhouses, they quickly spread outside. They will eat both dead and living plant material. In the UK, it's not clear whether they do notable damage to outdoor plants, but they have been problematic in New Zealand, so they are one to watch.

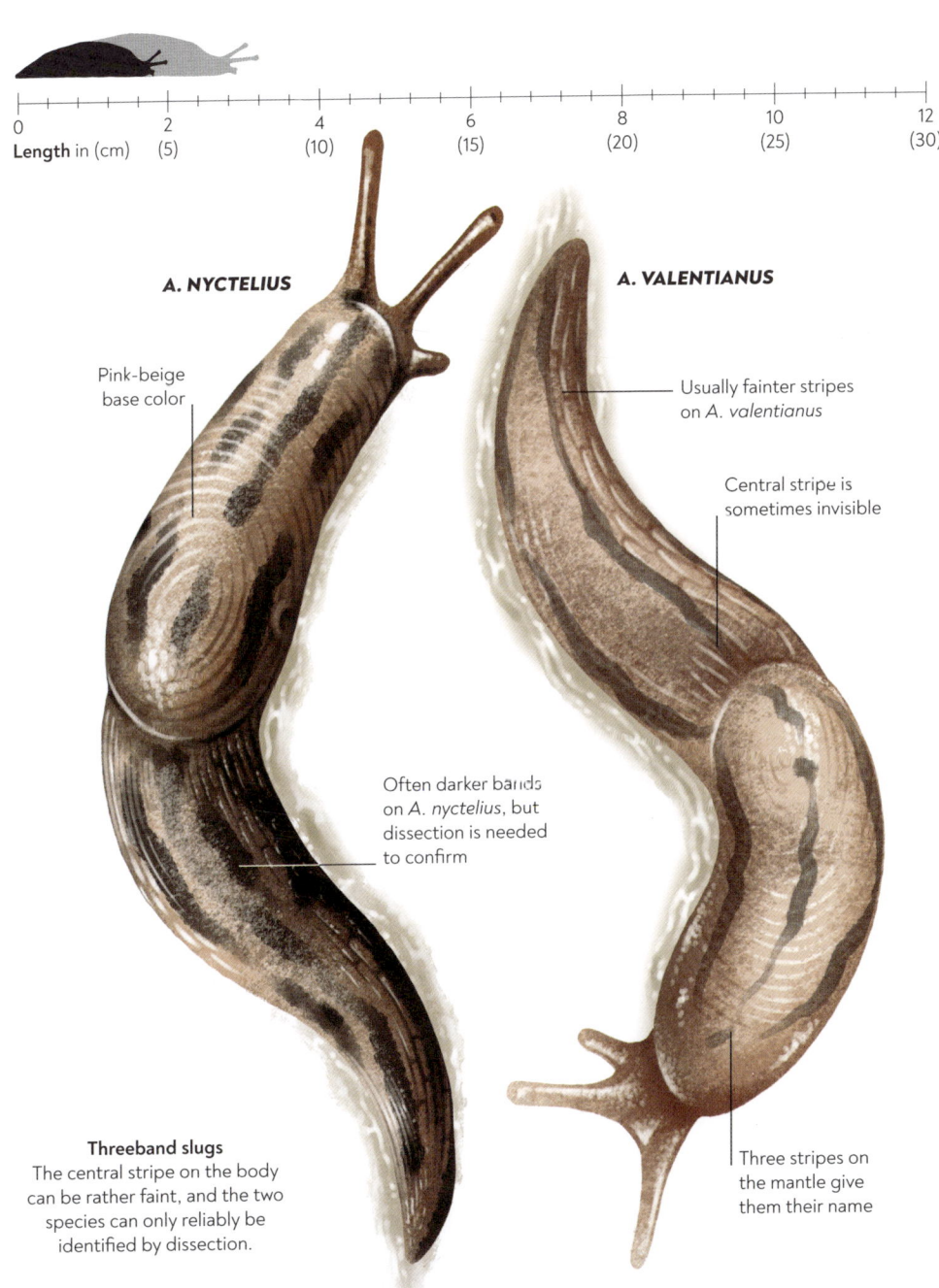

Length in (cm)

| 0 | 2 (5) | 4 (10) | 6 (15) | 8 (20) | 10 (25) | 12 (30) |

A. NYCTELIUS

A. VALENTIANUS

Pink-beige
base color

Usually fainter stripes
on *A. valentianus*

Central stripe is
sometimes invisible

Often darker bands
on *A. nyctelius*, but
dissection is needed
to confirm

Threeband slugs
The central stripe on the body
can be rather faint, and the two
species can only reliably be
identified by dissection.

Three stripes on
the mantle give
them their name

GRAY FIELD SLUG

Scientific name
Deroceras reticulatum

Family Agriolimacidae

Size 1⅜–2in (3.5–5cm)

Found Everywhere

Eats Garden plants and more

Identification
Medium difficulty

Color variations

The gray field slug is also known as the netted field slug, and this describes its key ID features—dark flecks, especially between the tubercles, make a "netted" pattern. It appears in shades of gray and beige, but as it is so common, it becomes easier to spot once you have identified a few. It also produces milky mucus, a feature unique to it and the rarer Arctic field slug, *Deroceras agreste*.

Although like most slugs it is omnivorous, it seems to prefer live material. It is well suited to temperate areas of the world, and it can reproduce more than once per year in the UK, usually in the spring and fall. This means that many of the individuals you encounter will be much smaller than adult size, ideal for hiding themselves inside heads of lettuce.

Friend or foe?

The gray field slug, despite being one of the smallest slugs, is the biggest problem species for cereal farmers, vegetable growers, and most likely for gardeners too. It is native to Western Europe but has spread to North America, New Zealand, and many other parts of the world. The silver lining to this is that there have been many studies on how to reduce its damage, including which natural predators, such as song thrushes (see p38), and parasites, such as nematodes (see p130), will feed on it.

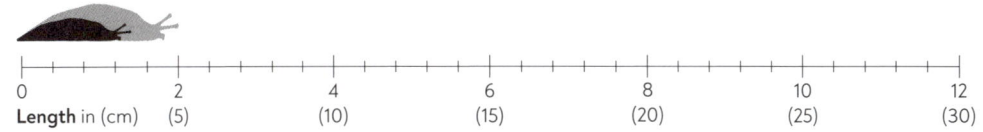

Length in (cm)

| 0 | 2 (5) | 4 (10) | 6 (15) | 8 (20) | 10 (25) | 12 (30) |

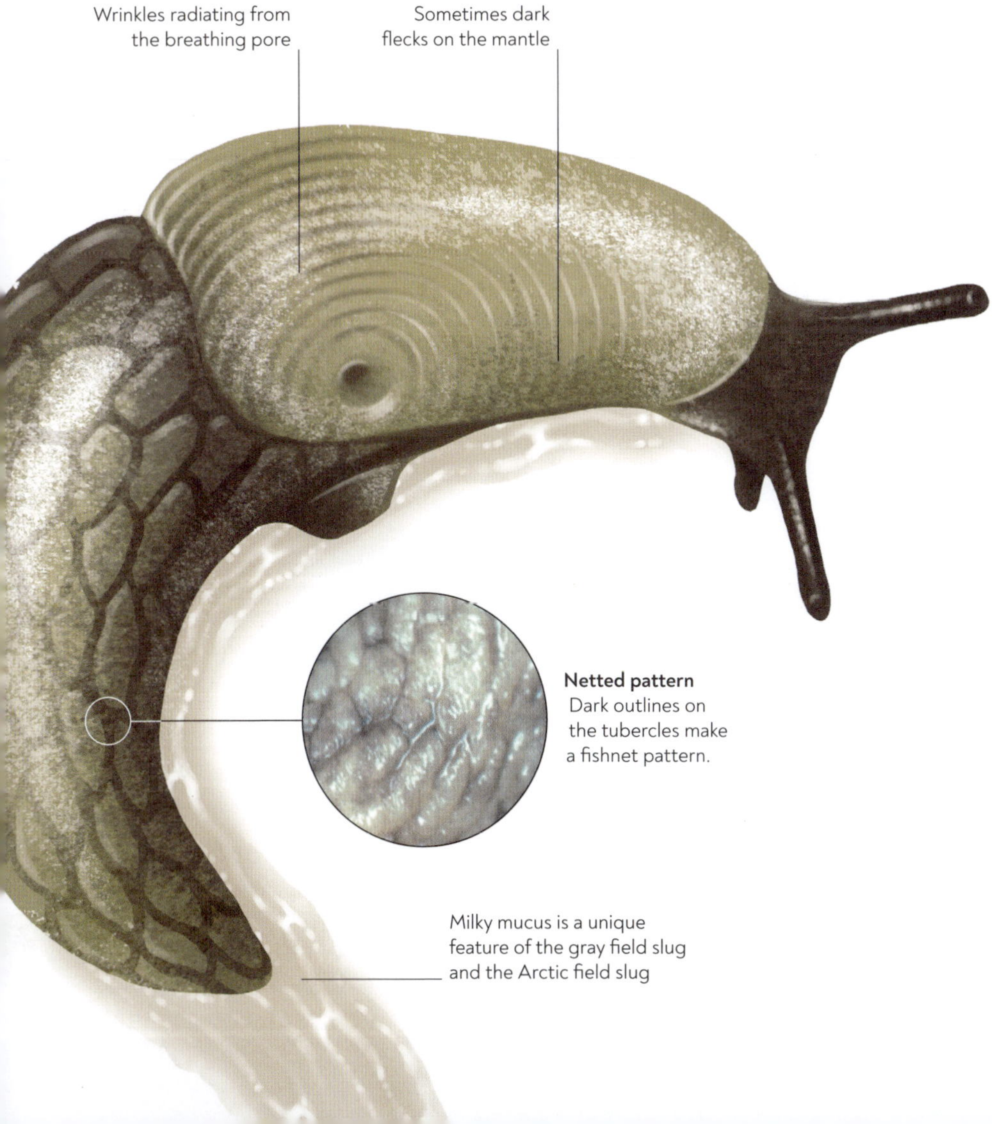

Wrinkles radiating from
the breathing pore

Sometimes dark
flecks on the mantle

Netted pattern
Dark outlines on
the tubercles make
a fishnet pattern.

Milky mucus is a unique
feature of the gray field slug
and the Arctic field slug

TRAMP SLUG

Scientific name
Deroceras invadens

Family Agriolimacidae

Size 1–1⅜in (2.5–3.5cm)

Found Urban areas, gardens, and farms

Eats Unknown

Identification Difficult

Color variations

Similar in appearance to the gray field slug (see p88), the tramp slug is usually darker with a blunter tail, and the edge of the breathing pore is noticeably pale. Its mantle is somewhat transparent, and the pale oval shape inside is its internal shell. It also looks very similar to the much rarer Sicilian slug, *Deroceras panormitanum*.

The clue in its species name, *invadens*, is that this is another slug that has successfully spread the world over from its likely origin in Italy. It seems to survive well in a range of habitats and climates, although it's not the most widespread slug in the world. One of the benefits of being a small slug is that it's easier to hide, including in the mud of a wheel well, vegetables for sale, or potted plants.

Friend or foe?
There's not a huge amount of evidence for this species causing substantial plant damage in Europe, but its impact on farms and gardens in New Zealand means it's another one to watch.

Steeply sloping tail

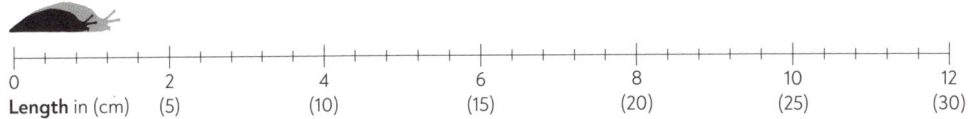

Length in (cm)   0   2 (5)   4 (10)   6 (15)   8 (20)   10 (25)   12 (30)

Internal shell
The internal shell is visible through the mantle skin as a pale oval.

Sometimes has tiny dark spots

Breathing pore has a distinct pale edge

Often darker in general than the gray field slug

The tramp slug has successfully spread the world over from its likely origin in Italy.

MARSH SLUG

Scientific name
Deroceras laeve

Family Agriolimacidae

Size ⅝–1in (1.5–2.5cm)

Found Many damp habitats

Eats Possibly plants in greenhouses

Identification
Medium difficulty

Color variations

A very small slug with a short tail, the marsh slug tends to have much warmer brown colors than the other *Deroceras* species. It also has more noticeable spaced-out concentric ridges on its mantle than the others. All of these little *Deroceras* slugs are hard to tell apart for the beginner, and a couple need dissection to confirm their identity.

The marsh slug gets its name from an association with very damp habitats such as wetlands, riverbanks, and boggy forests. It seems to be genuinely at home in water, surviving floods and even choosing to travel underwater. This is unusual among terrestrial slugs, which need to breathe air because they lack the gills of their marine ancestors. There are likely both native and introduced populations of this species in the US.

Friend or foe?
The marsh slug seems to eat both dead and live material, and has occasionally been noted causing problems for growers, particularly in greenhouses, on soft plant parts such as petals. On the other hand, there is at least one report of them eating mealybugs on a Cape primrose (*Streptocarpus*) in a greenhouse.

The marsh slug seems to be genuinely at home in water, surviving floods and even choosing to travel underwater.

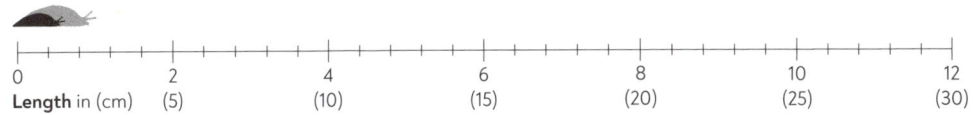

Length in (cm) 0 2 (5) 4 (10) 6 (15) 8 (20) 10 (25) 12 (30)

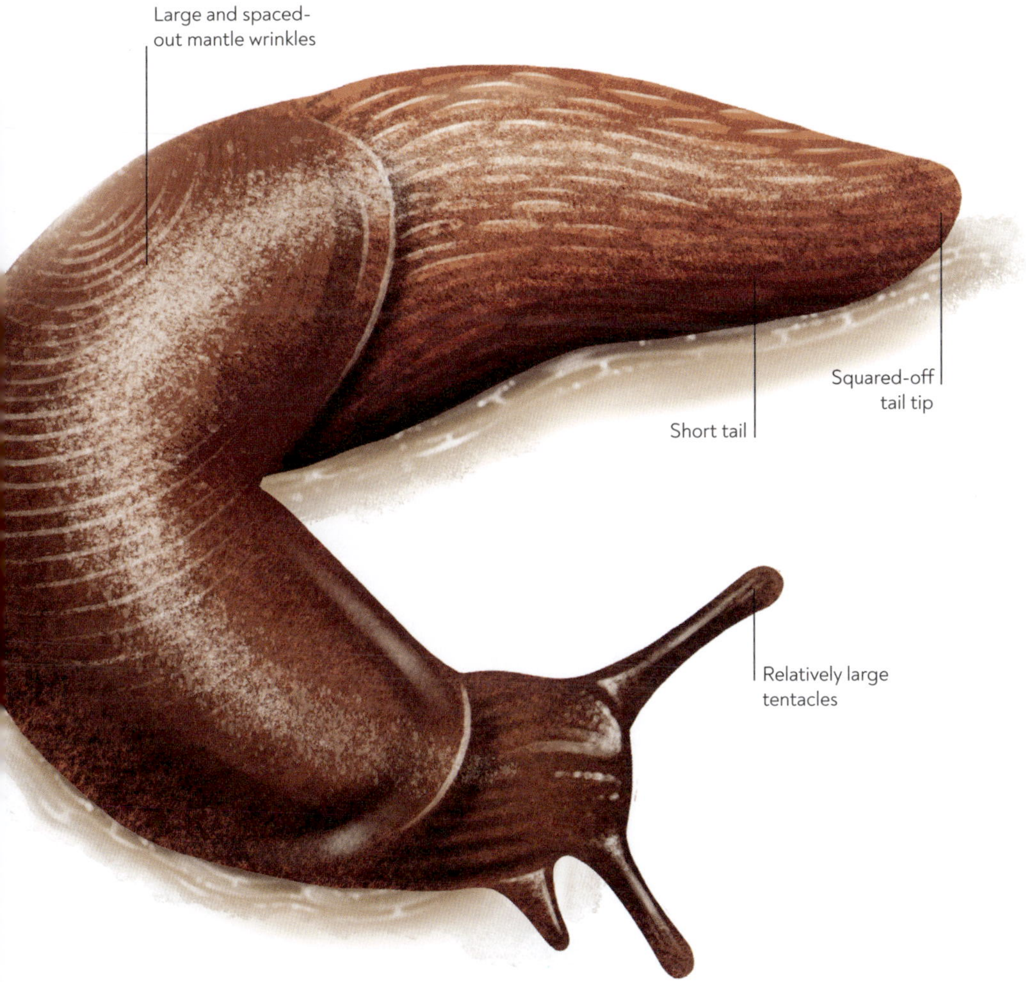

Large and spaced-out mantle wrinkles

Short tail

Squared-off tail tip

Relatively large tentacles

WORM SLUG

Scientific name
Boettgerilla pallens

Family Boettgerillidae

Size 1⅜–2¼in (3.5–5.5cm)

Found On US west coast, but uncommon

Eats Mostly rotting material

Identification Easy

Color variations

This is a long-keeled slug but in a different family from the others and quite unique. It is named for its long, thin, wormlike body shape, which is unmistakable and striking to see. It is usually white but sometimes pale gray with a darker tail tip. It is very delicate, as we found during the Slugs Count project (see pp44–45), where it rarely made it through the mail intact to be verified, no matter how securely packaged it was.

The worm slug lives almost entirely underground, often in earthworm burrows feeding on worm feces. It can wriggle its way down to depths of up to 2ft (60cm), but is usually found nearer the surface. A major study of this species was carried out by Gunn using a rhizotron, which is essentially an underground space with windows that lets scientists sit and make observations with minimal disturbance on the wild soil habitat.

Friend or foe?

The worm slug is mostly a detritivore, so it has minimal impact on humans, but it is another species that has spread from Europe around the world. It spread remarkably far and wide before really being noticed, perhaps because of its underground lifestyle.

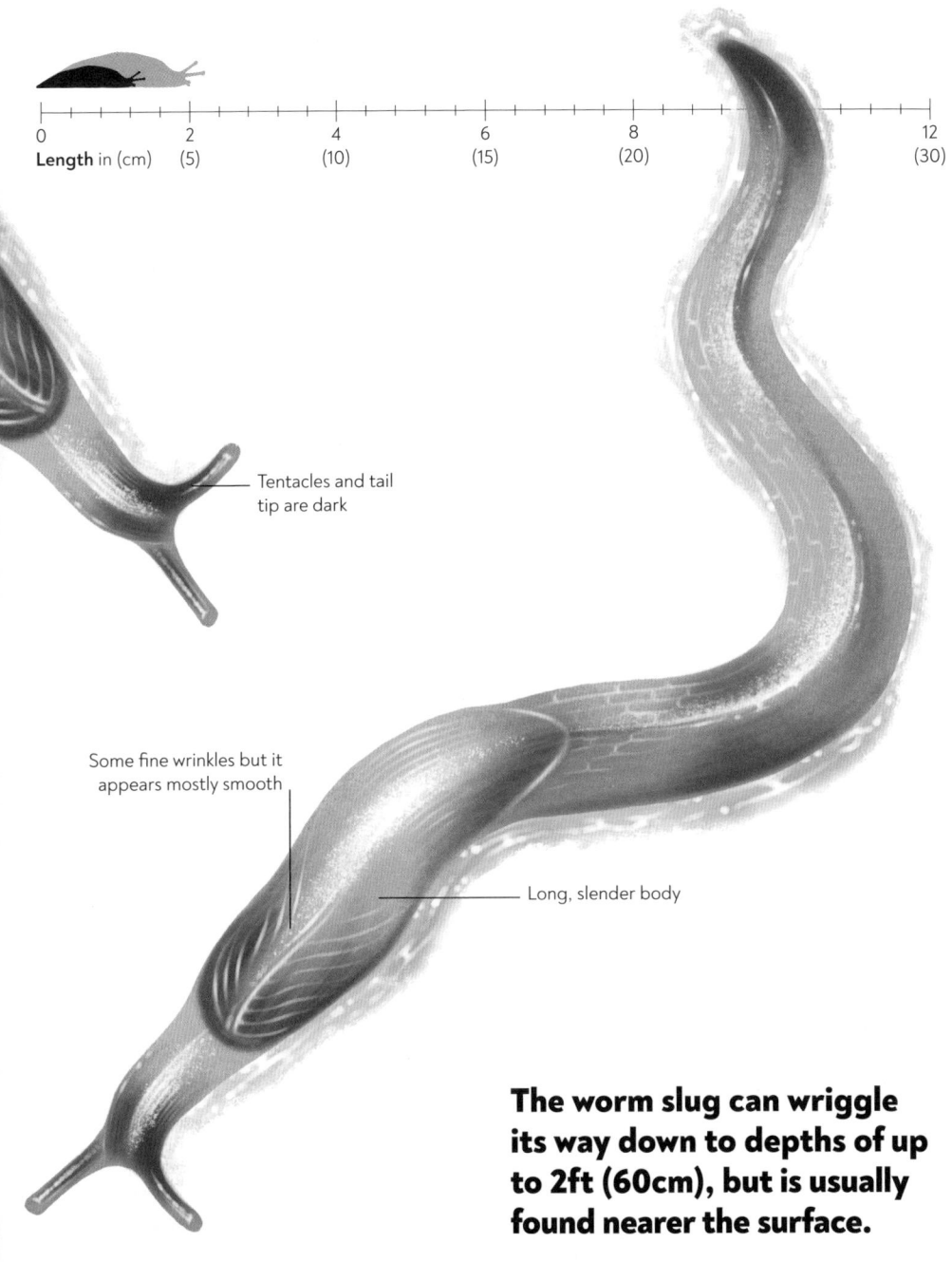

Length in (cm)

0 2 (5) 4 (10) 6 (15) 8 (20) 12 (30)

Tentacles and tail tip are dark

Some fine wrinkles but it appears mostly smooth

Long, slender body

The worm slug can wriggle its way down to depths of up to 2ft (60cm), but is usually found nearer the surface.

EAR SHELLED SLUG

Scientific name
Testacella haliotidea

Family Testacellidae

Size 2¾–4in
(7–10cm)

Found Gardens

Eats Earthworms

Identification
Medium difficulty

Color variations

Some slugs have external shells, and this is the one you are most likely to encounter in the garden, although it is fairly rare and mostly subterranean, so you will have to be lucky. There are four *Testacella* species in the UK, all with small, flattish shells on the tip of their tail. They look very different from most other slugs, having evolved from a snail ancestor independently (see p15). Their mantle is mostly hidden under the residual shell.

Shelled slugs are earthworm predators, slipping through the soil to hunt and eat the worms alive. The teeth on their radula are well suited for this purpose, being barbed to help drag the worm into their mouth.

Friend or foe?
They're not interested in your plants, but a predator of earthworms might be considered a negative in the garden, given earthworms are so important for soil structure. These rare and interesting slugs don't occur frequently, but where they have been introduced to the US, they could be a threat.

Shelled slugs look very different from most other slugs, having evolved from a snail ancestor independently.

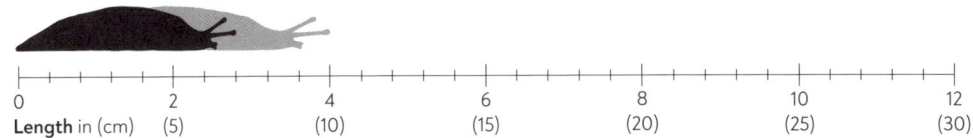

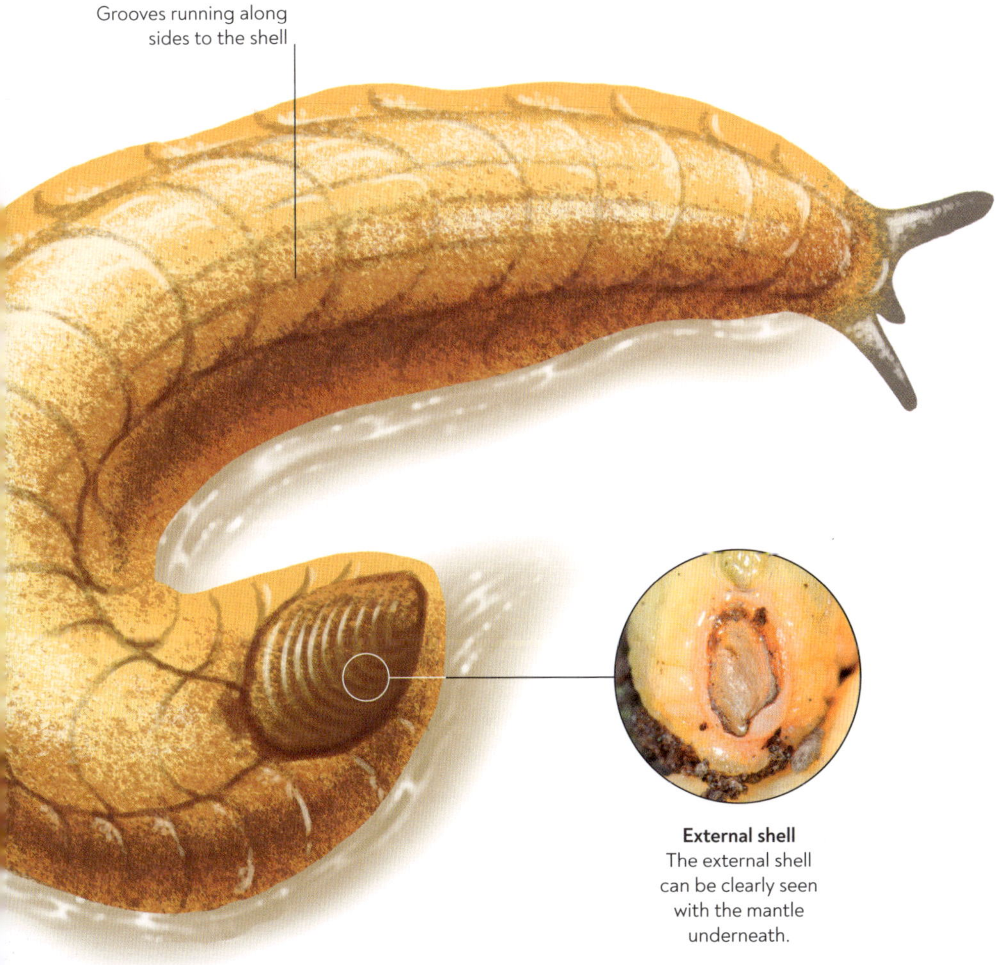

Length in (cm)

| 0 | 2 (5) | 4 (10) | 6 (15) | 8 (20) | 10 (25) | 12 (30) |

Grooves running along
sides to the shell

External shell
The external shell
can be clearly seen
with the mantle
underneath.

GHOST SLUG

Scientific name
Selenochlamys ysbryda

Family
Trigonochlamydidae

Size 2–3in (5–7.5cm)

Found Not found in the US; deep underground in gardens

Eats Earthworms

Identification Easy

Color variations

The ghost slug earns its name from its pale, somewhat pear-shaped body, and its face with reduced tentacles that lack eye spots. The mantle is just a small circle near the tail end, and its purplish internal organs can just be seen under the skin.

The ghost slug was discovered in a garden in Cardiff, Wales, in 2008 and had never been recorded before, so slug scientists Ben Rowson and Bill Symondson had to set about describing and naming it. Its appearance and mysterious origin led them to choose the common name "ghost." The slug is also special for having the Welsh language in its scientific name, with "*ysbryd*" meaning "ghost" or "spirit." The only other slugs in the same family are found in the Caucasus Mountains, between the Black Sea and the Caspian Sea. Since its discovery in the UK, the ghost slug has been found in Crimea (its likely native range), but it remains an enigmatic creature.

Friend or foe?

The ghost slug is even more rare and fascinating than the shelled slugs, so I hope it can be excused a few earthworms to munch. Despite its poor eyesight, it's a formidable predator, with teeth described as "spearhead-like points."

Mantle at tip of tail ———

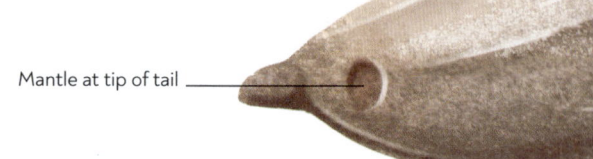

FRIEND OR FOE? | *Selenochlamys ysbryda*

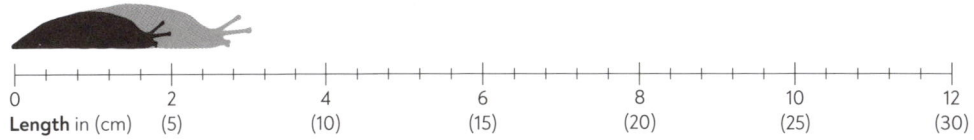

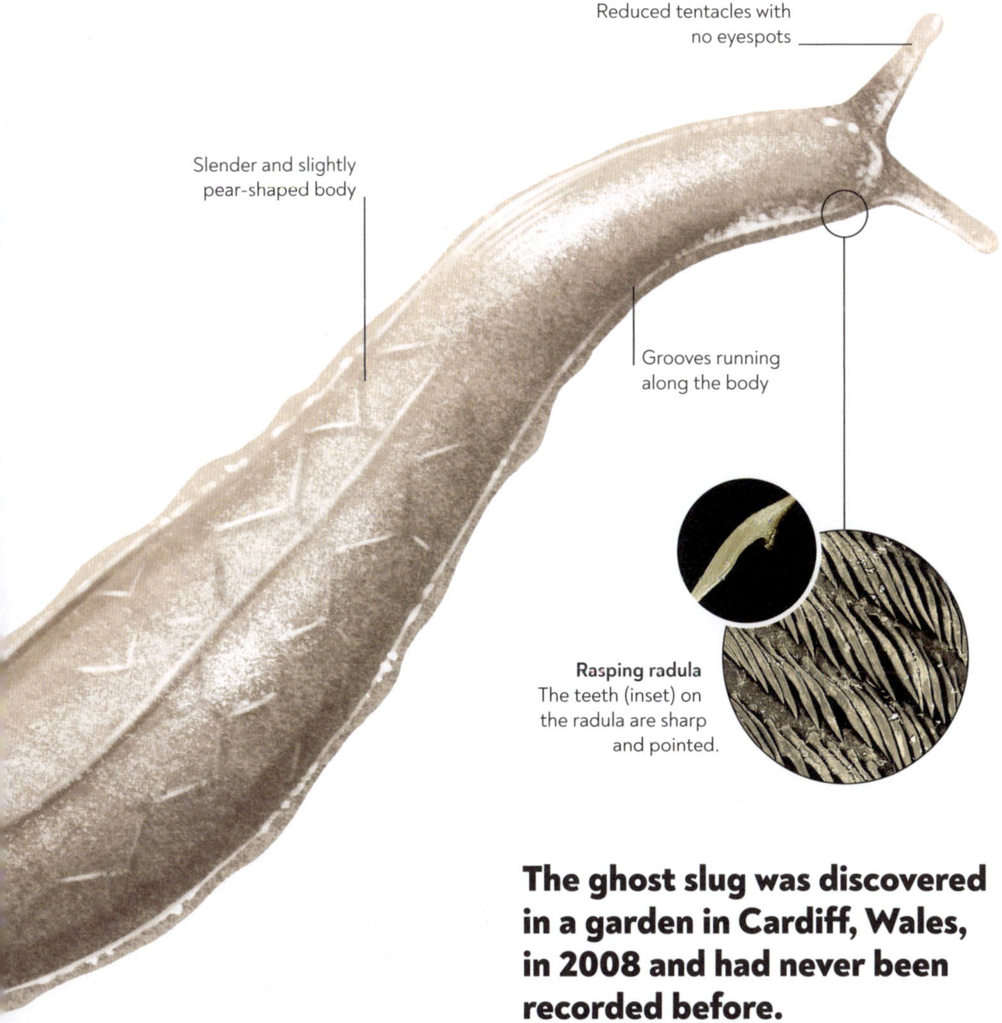

Length in (cm)

0

2 (5)

4 (10)

6 (15)

8 (20)

10 (25)

12 (30)

Reduced tentacles with
no eyespots

Slender and slightly
pear-shaped body

Grooves running
along the body

Rasping radula
The teeth (inset) on
the radula are sharp
and pointed.

**The ghost slug was discovered
in a garden in Cardiff, Wales,
in 2008 and had never been
recorded before.**

WINTER SEMI-SLUG

Scientific name
Vitrina pellucida

Family Vitrinidae

Size ½in (1cm)

Found Fields, roadsides, tundra

Eats Carnivorous

Identification
Medium difficulty

Color variations

This slug is most likely not to be recognized as a slug because it straddles the line between slugs and snails so thoroughly that it is often included in the snail list. It has a complete-looking coiled shell, but when it tries to hide, you can see why it is called a semi-slug—it can tuck its head in, but most of the body remains outside. The mantle actually overlaps the shell a bit, and the relative size of its shell means its body will not fit inside.

Its common name comes from the fact that full-grown adults are mostly seen in wintertime, but it is also known by the common name pellucid glass snail, with "pellucid" referring to the transparency of its shell.

Coiled shell _____

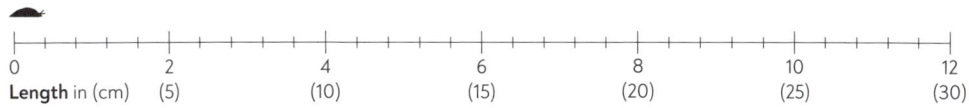

Length in (cm) 0   2 (5)   4 (10)   6 (15)   8 (20)   10 (25)   12 (30)

Its small size means it's tricky to find, and it would probably need some careful sifting of garden soil or rummaging to discover. Then you might need a magnifying glass to see its semi-slug features!

Friend or foe?
The winter semi-slug doesn't have many observations of its feeding habits—it may be carnivorous or a detritivore. If it does graze on live plants, it is too tiny and sparsely distributed to be noticeable.

The winter semi-slug has a complete-looking coiled shell, but its body does not fit inside.

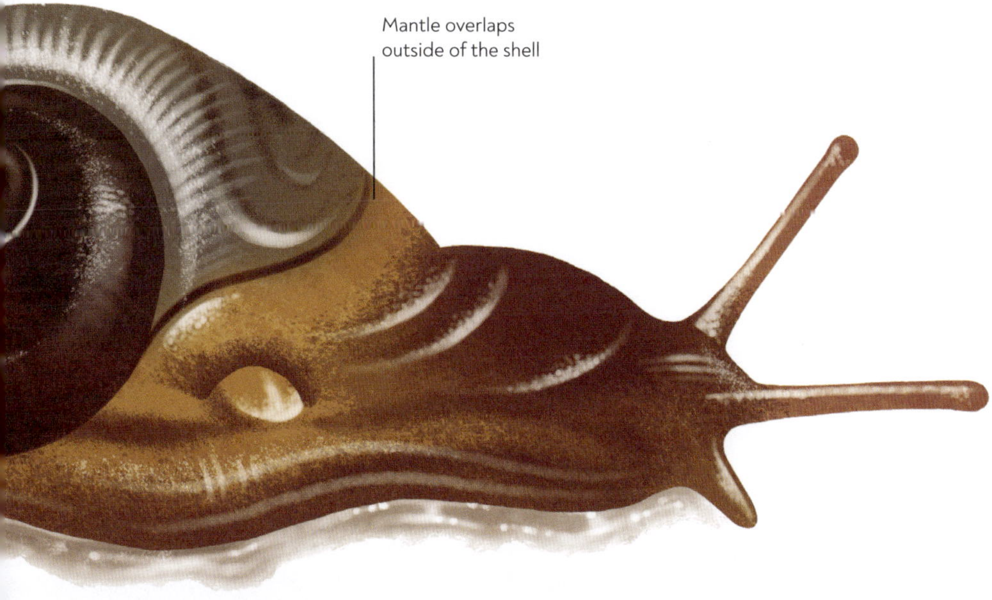

Mantle overlaps outside of the shell

What can gardeners do?

BATTLES OLD AND NEW

Gardeners have been battling with slugs for a very long time— the earliest mention of them as horticultural foes in the RHS Lindley Library collection is from *The Profitable Arte of Gardening* by Thomas Hill in 1568, where "against snayles, both with shell and without," he recommends adding fresh-pressed oil or soot to garden beds.

The problem with slugs

Frustration with slugs and snails continues to this day, and can be quantified by the inquiries we receive from members using the RHS Gardening Advice service. Questions relating to garden animals of any kind come to my team, and we record what the topic of inquiry was when we answer them. Of the 3,000 to 4,000 inquiries we answer each year, about 6.5 percent are about slugs and snails. In fact, they have been our most inquired-about topic for 12 of the last 20 years. The inquiries span diagnosis questions, such as "What's been making these holes in my plant?", to practical ones that ask specifically how to tackle slug problems.

Prevention past and present

Today, we haven't "solved" the problem of slugs in gardens. There is a vast array of prevention and control methods suggested, speculated on, or sold, but for many of these, there's no evidence for how well they work, especially the smaller-scale, home-garden techniques.

For example, the use of soot mentioned in Thomas Hill's book continued for some time but never gained real evidence for its effectiveness. Then it dropped out of fashion, perhaps because soot became a less common household resource as people stopped burning coal, or perhaps with the advent of pesticides.

Scientific research is usually carried out with agriculture, or at least commercial horticulture, in mind. In these settings, what is practical and profitable is much more restrictive because farmers and growers justifiably need to prioritize both crop yield and saleable quality. Consequently, the lower-labor options of biological controls (natural enemies that can be produced and sold) and chemical control (pesticides) dominate.

Home and community gardens, by contrast, benefit from a high availability of labor (that's you) and much more freedom and flexibility in plant choice and outcome. In the garden, we can make more use of cultural control options, such as plant choice and care, soil and water management, and repellents; and physical management, like trapping, removing by hand, or digging.

The scientific evidence for some of these is scarce, and occasionally anecdotal evidence can be spurious. Many, however, are worth trying, especially if they are low risk and cheap, and we'll look at a range of them in this chapter.

Throughout this, we must keep in mind that slugs are not simply a problem to be solved, but a vital member of the garden food chain, so our plant-protection activities should strive for a balanced system where slugs have their place.

Many cultural control options are worth trying in the garden, especially if they are low risk and cheap.

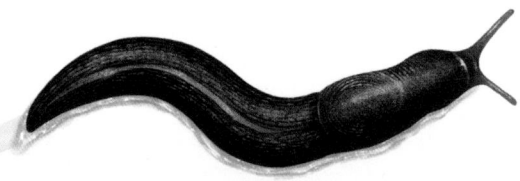

PESTICIDE PROBLEMS

The little blue pellets are a common sight on garden center shelves and sprinkled around gardens, but are they the answer to the battle with slugs and snails?

Past and present

The bright blue slug pellets that you may be familiar with contain the ingredient metaldehyde. They are very widely used around the world, but accidental poisonings of children and pets, and contamination of waterways, are common side effects. This led to them being banned in the UK in 2020, leaving ferric phosphate as the only legally available slug pellet for UK gardeners. Metaldehyde pellets are still available in the United States and the European Union (EU).

Ferric phosphate slug pellets are a paler blue with a naturally occurring active ingredient that makes them compatible with organic growing. This doesn't mean they are safe, however. There is already evidence that they are harmful to earthworms, which are beneficial in the garden ecosystem, and fish, and can be an irritant to humans.

If you do intend to use them, it's important to store them safely and apply them sparsely. The packaging is required to have guidance on application rate, which is usually that they be scattered thinly at $\frac{1}{6}$oz (5g) per 11 square feet (1 sq m), but unfortunately misuse or overapplication is still common.

The future

Professional growers are choosing and being encouraged to minimize pesticide use and move toward Integrated Pest Management (IPM; see opposite). This is a strategic approach that prioritizes cultural and biological methods.

Similarly, pesticide use by home gardeners is quite widespread but may now be decreasing. A survey by the Health and Safety Executive in 2019 found lower pesticide use than

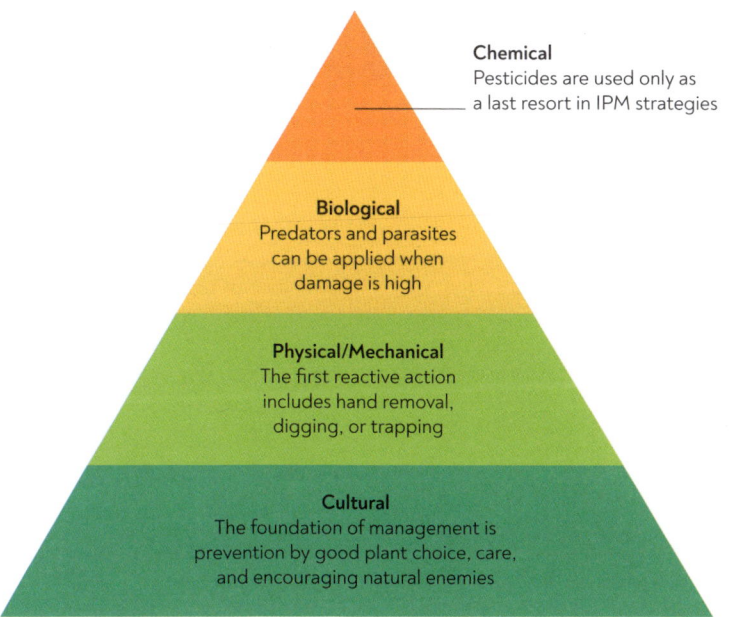

Chemical
Pesticides are used only as a last resort in IPM strategies

Biological
Predators and parasites can be applied when damage is high

Physical/Mechanical
The first reactive action includes hand removal, digging, or trapping

Cultural
The foundation of management is prevention by good plant choice, care, and encouraging natural enemies

in the 2016 survey, but still estimated 46 percent of UK gardeners were using slug pellets at that time (there is no similar survey for the US). Since the metaldehyde withdrawal, many will have switched to ferric phosphate, but I see an ever-growing sentiment among gardeners that pesticides are not the answer.

The need to move away from pesticides becomes more pressing as we face up to the looming biodiversity crisis. With 30 percent of UK urban areas covered by gardens, we are in an ideal position

Integrated Pest Management (IPM)
The IPM pyramid shows the foundation of pest management should be preventative, with reactive measures focusing on the least environmental risk.

to have a positive effect by providing habitats where humans and wildlife can coexist. For our friends (and foes), the slugs, movement toward tolerance or even appreciation for their role in the ecosystem will help with this positive outcome.

CHOOSING THE RIGHT PLANTS

If your garden has a thriving slug population, you may have to abandon the plan for a hosta collection and curate a less slug-appealing planting plan.

Slug loves

As we saw in Chapter 2, many garden slugs are simultaneously very omnivorous and pretty choosy (see p36). In our RHS Gardening Advice service inquiries about slugs, we also record which plant was involved wherever possible. Over time, we have recorded slug or snail damage on nearly 300 different plant types.

There are lots of vegetables in our data, especially potatoes, which is not surprising: it is so frustrating to go to harvest and discover that something has already eaten your crop!

Slug (and snail) top 10

Here are the top 10 slug and snail favorites from our data. The caveat here is that our records show what we are asked about, not necessarily what is most eaten in the garden.

Host plant	% of slug/snail inquiries
1 Potato	6.6%
2 Magnolia	5.9%
3 Daffodil	4.7%
4 Hosta	4.3%
5 Dahlia	3.6%
6 Clematis	3.0%
7 Pepper	2.5%
8 Brassica	2.4%
9 Runner bean	2.2%
10 Iris	1.9%
Other named plants	62.9%

Slug loathes

There are generally two reasons why slugs avoid certain plants: either the plant is too tricky to eat with a radula, or there are high levels of a plant-defense chemical (see p36).

ABOVE Ornamental grasses are often safe from nibbling by slug herbivores.

RIGHT Although they have furry leaves, I've often seen *Senecio candidans* ANGEL WINGS with the fuzz grazed away by slugs (inset).

Slug grazing can create beautiful patterns

Shrubs and other woody plants are often safe, as generally are plants with tough, waxy, or furry leaves. Mature grasses frequently remain unnibbled, which is most likely due to a high silica content.

For ornamental herbaceous plants, the RHS website has a list of plants that are less likely to be eaten by slugs and snails (see p139).

Resistant varieties

Among plants that we want to grow despite their slug susceptibility, a few have resistant varieties. Many hostas are marketed in this way, although it is widely known that they are less palatable to slugs, rather than being truly resistant. For example, hosta grower Bowdens advertises 22 of 49 varieties as slug resistant in their 2024 printed catalog.

Potatoes are the only plant group with slug-resistant varieties that have more scientifically robust trials backing them up, such as the cultivars 'Pentland Dell' and 'Majestic'. The effect is most likely due to properties of the skin, with less susceptible varieties having smoother skin at a microscopic level and a different taste.

TIME AND PLACE

You can tailor your gardening calendar and layout to avoid the worst of slug attention. Mild and damp weather is when slugs are most active, and so you might consider various plant-protection strategies, particularly in spring and fall. If you like more precision, there is a SlugWatch app where you can enter your postcode to get a traffic light slug forecast.

Timing matters

To avoid holey potatoes, timing is key, and the earlier potatoes are harvested, the less they are likely to be nibbled. Slug damage can increase up to 10-fold between late summer and mid-fall.

This increase in damage from late summer may be because of the slug life cycle (see pp16–19), as juveniles have reached maturity by then, and weather conditions become damper, which slugs prefer. It may also be due to properties of the potatoes themselves, with earlies having less appealing skin, and late-season potatoes getting steadily more attractive once they are mature.

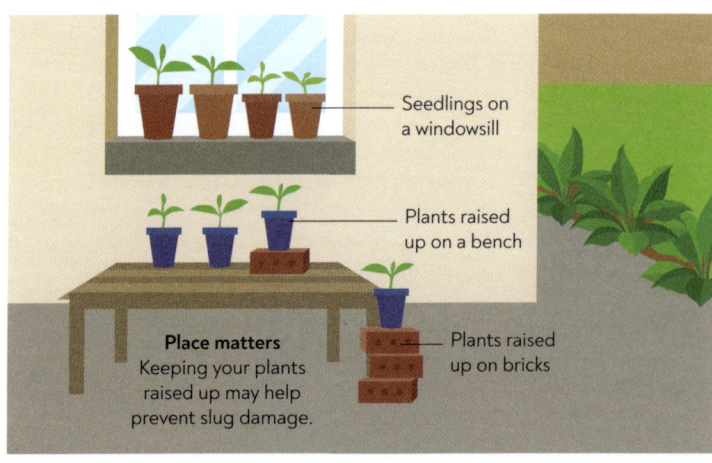

Seedlings on a windowsill

Plants raised up on a bench

Plants raised up on bricks

Place matters
Keeping your plants raised up may help prevent slug damage.

Growing seedlings outdoors but raised off the ground on a table or bench can help prevent slug damage.

Sensitive seedlings

Seedlings are one of a plant's most vulnerable life stages—they are soft and easy to nibble, and often coincide with damp springtime when slugs are roaming happily. Growing seedlings on a windowsill or in a greenhouse will help protect them at the tiny stage.

If you don't have indoor space, or the plants prefer it cooler, growing them outdoors but raised off the ground on a table or bench can help. When the food is farther away, slugs are less likely to travel up a table leg, and even more so if the leg has a copper barrier around it (see p117). If direct sowing is necessary, then seedlings may need other protective measures (see pp132–33) until they grow larger and more robust.

Tidy or messy?

There are opposing schools of thought about how much garden maintenance to do. Agricultural advice says to minimize weeds, crop residues, and organic matter to reduce hiding places and food sources. An alternative strategy is to leave rotting organic matter, weeds, or sacrificial plants for omnivorous slugs to feed on. My inclination is toward messiness.

The Agriculture and Horticulture Development Board (AHDB) says that slug damage is greater near field perimeters, where there are hedges and mixed vegetation as a refuge for slugs. But in most gardens, the whole site is more like these field edges, so we are dealing with a very different scenario, and it is not practical to minimize all slug food sources.

In my experience of slug-prone areas with lots of bare soil, the few plants there get clobbered. In contrast, where vegetation is dense and varied, the holey leaves are at least less noticeable.

There is also evidence for the benefits of heterogeneous (mixed tidy/messy) habitats in encouraging ground beetles and other natural enemies of slugs (see pp124–25). However, for fruit and vegetable growing, the inherent tidiness of crop cultivation necessitates a more complex strategy (see pp132–33).

SOIL AND WATER

Soil and water are fundamental elements of the garden and play an important role in the ecology of slugs, so can we channel them to our advantage?

Dig for victory?

In general, slugs are more numerous on moist, medium-coarse clay soil with plenty of organic matter and soil pores to hide in. Gardeners with sandy soils, such as at RHS Garden Wisley, may find that slugs are not as numerous. The addition of organic matter can make a more inviting environment for slugs, as it provides both a moist, friable shelter and a potential source of food. However, this is not a reason to avoid organic fertilizers in gardens because our omnivorous slug species will help digest them to make the nutrients more available for the plants.

In an agricultural setting, rotovating has been shown to reduce numbers of slugs, in some cases by more than two-thirds. Turning the soil to expose slugs and their eggs to predators such as birds may, therefore, help reduce their population. Another study in a more horticultural setting tried to capitalize on this by hand hoeing weeds twice a week, but this didn't reduce slug damage.

Before we abandon aspirations of no dig and return to rototilling, it's worth mentioning that even scientists from the 1970s noted that the overcultivation and compaction of the soil by such intensive processes can have downsides for soil and plant health.

It is unfortunate that conditions that are good for plant growth are also good for slugs. But we can embrace this and provide the best conditions for healthy plants to grow strong enough to withstand a bit of nibbling.

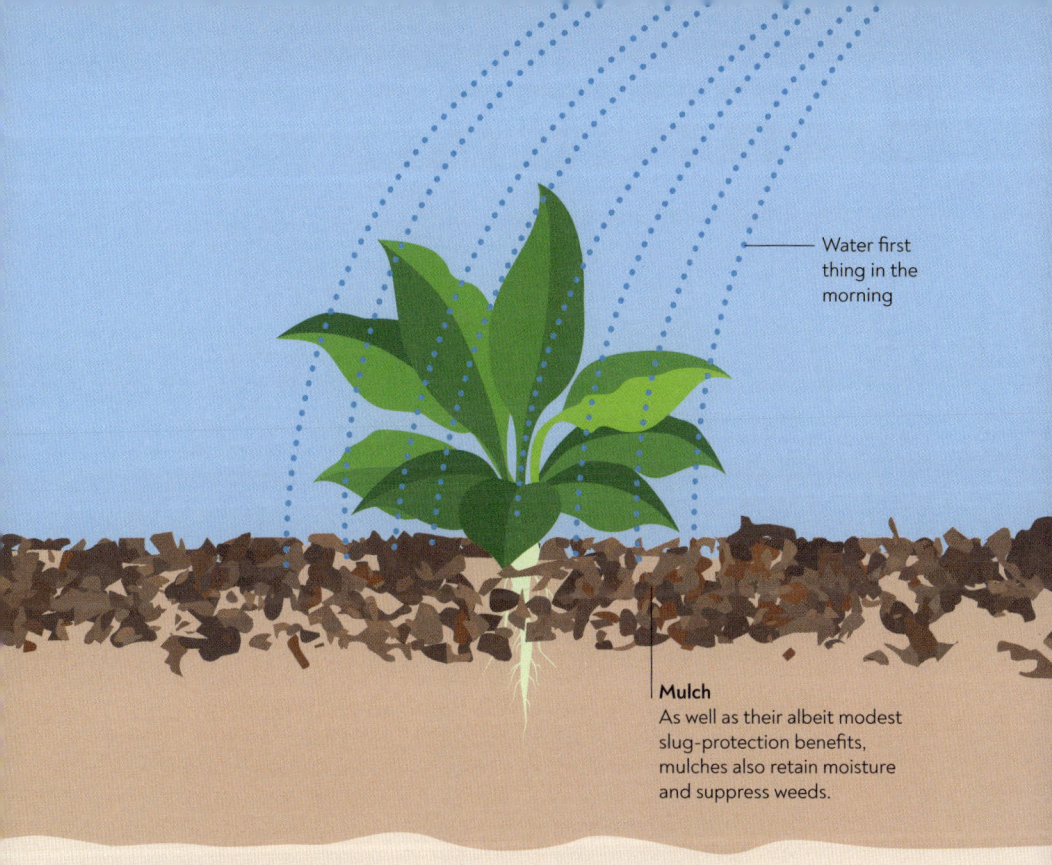

Water first
thing in the
morning

Mulch
As well as their albeit modest
slug-protection benefits,
mulches also retain moisture
and suppress weeds.

Moisture management

We can use our understanding
of slugs' biology to our advantage.
Slug activity is highly dependent on
soil moisture, and slugs are nocturnal,
so watering in the morning rather
than the evening means the water
is less available on the surface to
provide ideal slug-roaming
conditions around your plants.
One study found switching from
evening to morning watering
provided equivalent protection
to an application of metaldehyde
slug pellets.

Mulches

I tested combinations of nematode
biological control (see p130) with
a straw-based mulch, which, even
by itself, resulted in a small reduction
in damage and did not impact the
effectiveness of the nematodes.
A wood-based mulch was also
effective as a deterrent to slug
movement and plant damage in
some laboratory studies.

Even if slug-protection benefits
are modest, mulches suppress weeds
and retain moisture in the soil, so
they are definitely worth investing in.

BARRIERS

Some organic substances are suggested as a form of physical control for use around plants to deter the slugs from reaching the foliage.

Eggshells

Eggshells, crumbled up and sprinkled in a circle around the base of a plant, are a deterrent that many gardeners swear by. The idea is that the sharp edges will cause discomfort or pain to the slug's soft underbelly, and they will be repelled. Unfortunately, this one doesn't stand up to much scrutiny. Despite it being mentioned regularly in gardening literature and in passing in scientific reviews, I have found no published study testing the effectiveness of eggshells as a barrier.

I decided to do a trial of this and a few other commonly suggested barriers on lettuce in raised beds at the RHS field research facility. After six weeks of lettuce growth, none of the barriers tested provided any reduction in slug nibbling at all (see p119). This isn't an unexpected result because slugs and snails have very complex mucus on the sole of their foot that provides a lot of protection. They can make more mucus and change its composition as needed (see p30), so even if a surface is dry, sharp, or otherwise unpleasant, slugs and snails will be able to cross.

There are even videos on the internet showing snails crawling up and over a razor blade with no ill effects (search for them, I dare you!). If whatever is on the other side is attractive enough to motivate them to cross, they will.

Another mark against eggshells is their high calcium content, which might actually make them attractive to slugs and snails that need a source of dietary calcium to build their shells (as we've seen, even slugs have a shell). In fact, eggshells are often recommended as a calcium food source for pet giant African land snails. To pile on the counter-evidence, if there is any residual egg on the shells, this could also be attractive to the omnivorous species of slug.

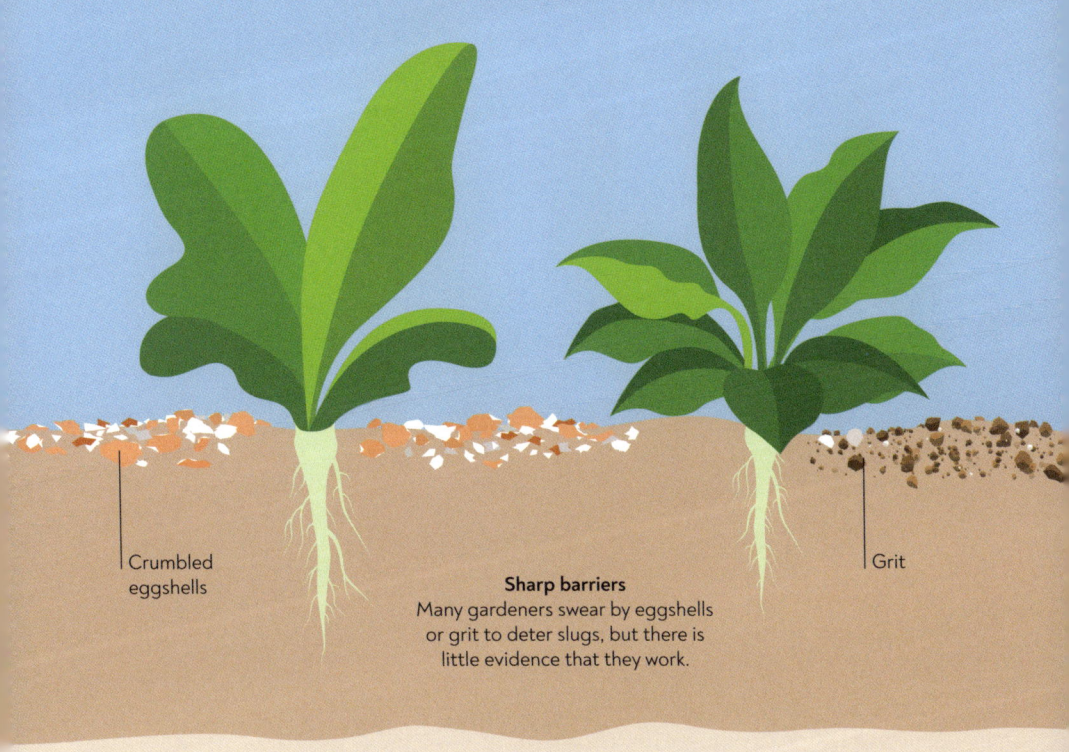

Crumbled
eggshells

Sharp barriers
Many gardeners swear by eggshells
or grit to deter slugs, but there is
little evidence that they work.

Grit

Grit, gravel, and sand

Other barriers that rely on being
sharp or rough, such as grit, gravel,
or sand, are likely to be similarly
ineffective. However, this assumption
is based on them being applied
in a circle around the plant base,
and broader mulches can be more
helpful (see p113).

That being said, if a mulch or
barrier has a mild deterrent effect,
it may be possible to reinforce it by
either decreasing the attractiveness
of the plant or increasing the size
of the barrier. For example, a top
dressing of grit combined with a

longer distance to overcome, such
as a plant in a pot, may prove more
effective. However, the drainage
holes can provide a shortcut, so
mesh or free-draining fabric inside
the pots might also be needed.

Deterrent barriers such as grit,
gravel, and sand are the holy grail
of slug and snail management, as
they don't involve killing the creatures,
just deterring them, and this topic
merits much more scientific research.
I would recommend testing and
trialing more inexpensive barriers
in your garden, even if there is no
scientific evidence for them working.

Copper foil can be attached to a pot, raised bed, or bench leg

Copper collars can be put around plants in the soil

Heavy metals
Many metals and their salts are deterrents to slugs and snails, and they can be incorporated into barriers and material design choices.

Galvanized zinc planters are a decorative way to deter slugs

There are a few heavy-metal repellents or barriers that do have some promise in the slug-exclusion strategy.

Copper

Copper is one of the few deterrents that has a decent body of evidence behind it. The mechanism by which copper works against slugs and snails is likely to be the deterrent and mild toxic effects of copper salts. In general, the larger the barrier, the more of a deterrent it could be.

Two widely available formats are copper tape to attach around pots, and copper collars to place around plants in the ground. Copper foil has been shown to be a useful barrier, although not an impenetrable one, in laboratory studies.

One study by Schüder et al. found that a 1¼in-(3cm-) wide strip of copper foil laid flat on the ground could stop 25 percent of *Deroceras* slugs crossing and 80 percent of snails (*Oxyloma elegans*, a small species). Watz & Nyqvist found that with a copper foil barrier of 2½in (6cm), the vulgar slug was delayed but not prevented from crossing.

Copper collars as such don't seem to have published studies,

but in my trial, they did not successfully reduce damage (see p119). This may be because of the major downside of copper collars: they don't go deep enough to prevent slugs from traveling underground and popping up inside.

Copper may be worth pursuing, but the format does need some further exploration, something I hope to test in the future. For now, it is worth trying where you can to factor in the distance, such as around pots, bench legs, or raised bed edges. However, examine copper tape products closely, as I have seen some that suspiciously never tarnish. If these have been laminated for shininess, it would negate the copper benefits.

Zinc and lead

Other heavy metals such as zinc and lead are also displeasing to slugs and may therefore act as a deterrent. As with copper, zinc has been recommended for a long time. Hall, in 1932, wrote: "For small upstanding plants, such as zinnia and dahlia seedlings, a collar of sheet zinc about one inch high is an absolute deterrent, and does not require renewal."

Here are a few more of the wide assortment of barriers and deterrents that are suggested for use against slugs, and their evidence, or lack of.

Coffee

Although employed by a number of gardeners, and with several coffee shops and supermarkets making their waste coffee grounds available, this approach needs some caution.

The repellent properties of coffee grounds may have something to do with caffeine, a neat solution of which was found to be an effective repellent to slugs and snails even at very low concentrations. But it was also lethal at higher concentrations, so fresh coffee and neat caffeine fall into a category of "needs safety testing" (see p120), especially as caffeine can also be toxic to insects and other animals.

Horgan et al. went into depth testing coffee grounds as a top-dressing repellent for four slug species. They found that coffee grounds that had composted for around eight months both reduced slug feeding and promoted plant growth. Older grounds promoted plant growth but had no effect on slugs, and fresher coffee grounds reduced slug feeding but also inhibited plant growth. So use with care, especially considering the possible toxic effects of caffeine.

Diatomaceous earth and dry silica

Diatomaceous earth is a crumbled rock made from fossilized algae that has grown in prominence as a physical control method for a range of insects and other organisms. With a high silica content, its mode of action is desiccation.

It might seem promising for our moisture-dependent slugs, but it doesn't seem to work in practice, possibly because it needs to remain in a dry setting, which is not practical as plants need to be watered.

Sodium silicate (also known as waterglass) showed some promise in a lab study, but a calcium silicate product was not very effective in a field study.

Seaweed

There is no trace of evidence in the scientific literature, but a product containing dried granulated seaweed was the most effective barrier in a *Which?* gardening trial. Perhaps the

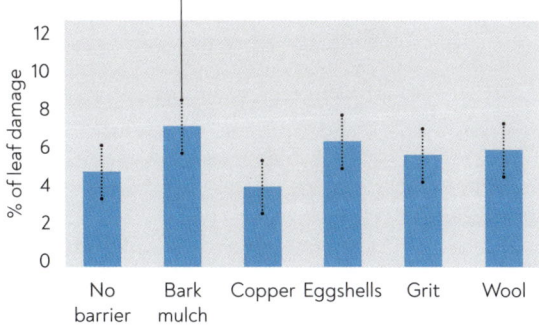

saltiness is displeasing to slugs, but it doesn't seem like the saltiness is a risk to the plants because seaweed has widespread use as a fertilizer.

Weed-suppressant matting

Often used in fruit and veg growing settings, these can reduce the number of slugs coming up from underground. Conversely, they aren't very attractive and are made of plastic, which should be minimized in the garden because of its cost to the environment.

Wood ash

This is the closest I can find for the soot mentioned in historical slug control (see p104). Some forms of wood ash may have a toxic outcome when sprinkled on slugs, but used as a barrier in an outdoor setting, they did not have a real effect.

Wool

In my trial (see chart right), the wool pellets had no effect after six weeks, but early on, it did look like they were protective. Over time, the fertilizing effects of wool may have caused the lettuce to overhang the barrier, so this one is worth a try, especially as wool does seem to have some repellent effect.

Electric fences

Several enterprising gardeners have suggested this deterrent to me, even including photos of their homemade set-up in action. It does have promise, and a couple of studies have successfully implemented it in a laboratory or polytunnel.

However, many may find installing a fence impractical. If using one, I would advise extreme caution and low voltage to avoid any risk to people, pets, and other animals.

The confidence interval lines show the range of statistical uncertainty in the measured leaf damage. Here, the lines indicate that there is no significant difference between the different barriers

Slug/snail barrier trial

I tested the effectiveness of slug/snail barriers applied around lettuces grown in outdoor beds for six weeks. The chart shows there was no statistically significant reduction in damage by any of the barriers compared to no barrier.

FOLIAR DETERRENTS

Some gardeners use foliar deterrents to deter slugs. Garlic, for example, is often recommended as a homemade spray to make leaves unpalatable to slugs, but, as we'll see, it may not be such a good idea.

Garlic and friends

Garlic solution is widely endorsed, especially by hosta growers, as a homemade spray to apply to plant leaves to repel slugs. There are studies showing that it can work as a repellent, so this may seem like a cheap and easy win, but it's actually not something that I recommend.

The problem is that garlic, even at fairly low concentrations, has been shown not only to cause high levels of mortality to the slugs themselves but also to other organisms, including ones that are beneficial.

This means it strays into the realm of homemade pesticides—something that I would never recommend because it is not possible to know what dosage is safe for use and what side effects may occur. In the UK, the Health and Safety Executive (HSE) advises against home remedies and notes that, in some cases, their use may be illegal.

However, the evidence for slugs detesting garlic means it may be useful as a companion plant, a strategy that doesn't seem to have been tested scientifically yet but one I hope to pursue in the future.

Another possible companion is cilantro, which has been shown to be a deterrent in the lab but was not corroborated in a field experiment.

Other plants that have been shown to work as molluscicides in their essential oil format, such as thyme, mint, and rosemary, could also hold promise as companion plants.

Boosting plant defenses

Although silica hasn't been shown to work as a physical barrier, there is some evidence that it can deter slug feeding when used as a fertilizer to boost the leaf silica content. This is in line with our understanding of slug plant preferences and natural plant defenses (see p36).

Despite extensive scientific study of calcium as a plant-defense chemical, it doesn't seem to have translated to evidence that calcium enrichment can help deter slugs. There has been a start to this in a study that looked at deterrence of caterpillars, but calcium enrichment didn't have a deterrent effect in a small lab study conducted by RHS summer student Emma Thornton, or in a study using wheat seedlings.

Plant oils
Increasingly, there are studies showing the repellent effects of various plant oils, such as cedarwood, birch tar, and myrrh, but many of these are also being investigated for molluscicidal action. Again, as these venture more into the realms of pesticides, I think we should avoid them, or at least wait for further science and ideally product-safety testing before trying them in the garden.

The essential oils of some herbs can be deterrents to slugs, including rosemary (above right), garden mint (right), and thyme (far right).

The essential oils of thyme, mint, and rosemary have been shown to work as molluscicides, and could be promising companion plants.

WARM-BLOODED SLUG ENEMIES

Now we start to get into the less slug-friendly options for protecting plants, but still on the wildlife-friendly track, by inviting in the slug predators. It's not as simple as sending a summons, but there are things you can do to encourage and support them.

Shrews

These little mouselike creatures with excessively pointy noses might dig a few small holes in your yard, but on the balance, they are more beneficial than harmful because they eat slugs and other insects.

Instead of working to eradicate them from your garden, you can support them by providing places for them to shelter such as log piles, compost heaps, or buried wooden hibernacula (shelters for winter). Also avoid pesticide use, including using anti-parasitic medicines on pets.

Other mammals

Many of the other slug-eating mammals, such as badgers, foxes, rats, shrews, and moles, are not necessarily creatures that we want to encourage in the garden, as they can create problems such as digging up flowerbeds or grass. But if you have a larger plot with more wild space, then some of them may be doing their part to balance slug populations.

Wild birds

There's a huge amount of bird advice to be found, so here are just a couple of tips:
- Birds may nest in your hedges and trees, so don't trim during nesting season, which generally is from February to August, and consider providing large nest boxes with round holes for birds such as little owls and starlings.

- You can offer supplementary food to entice birds in, but remember to wash feeders regularly to avoid spreading diseases. Thrushes like to eat fruit such as bruised apples and pears, in addition to slugs and snails.

Domestic birds

Chickens and ducks could be your personal slug-consuming army, but while they are often suggested for this purpose, there's not much evidence for how reliable they are.

Chickens have started to be used with some success as pest control in orchards. You might want to try this if you have enough space and would enjoy their company, but note that they are a big commitment and may sometimes peck plants and scratch in flowerbeds.

COLD-BLOODED SLUG ENEMIES

Making a wildlife-friendly garden to encourage reptile, amphibian, and invertebrate predators is likely to be a very satisfying strategy. One of the main benefits of promoting natural predators is that they help us build an ecosystem where slugs sustain their roles as recyclers and prey, but are reduced in number so our favorite plants are less damaged. We're not trying to exterminate slugs—natural enemies won't eradicate their prey completely—but rather reach a balanced population dynamic.

Frogs and toads

Adding a pond is a sure-fire way to invite these slug-eaters in, and it doesn't necessarily need to be a large pond. The common frog can use almost any pond, preferring shallow, still areas, whereas the common toad favors more open water. An ideal pond has a warm location, gently sloping sides with a range of depths and an irregular shape, and plenty of aquatic plants and surrounding vegetation.

You can also help sustain your frog and toad population by providing a damp but frost-protected hibernaculum, but they are likely to find their own in a log pile or

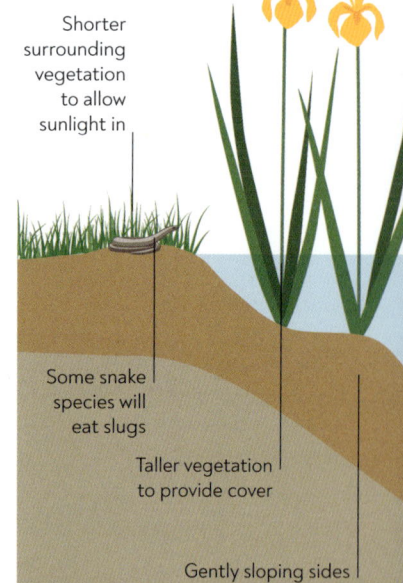

Shorter surrounding vegetation to allow sunlight in

Some snake species will eat slugs

Taller vegetation to provide cover

Gently sloping sides

compost heap. Finally, forgo bringing in koi (carp); fish are major predators of amphibian eggs and tadpoles.

Ground beetles
These small but mighty predators are one of the most extensively studied examples of natural herbivore control. In general, they prefer varied herbaceous settings, so diverse planting that tolerates a few weeds and has consistent groundcover may tempt them. However, many larger species are able to roam quite far away from cover, and so can be helpful even in a vegetable patch where there is more bare soil.

Avoid rototilling or heavy digging, especially in the spring, although the beetles can tolerate hand weeding. You'll notice that this somewhat contradicts the advice about digging to reduce slugs (see p112)!

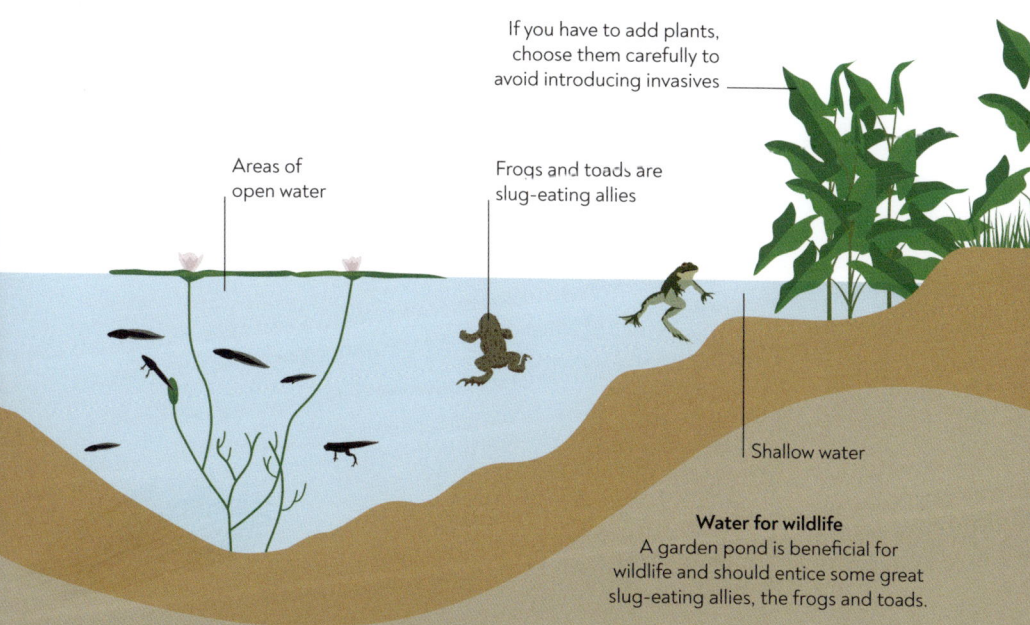

If you have to add plants, choose them carefully to avoid introducing invasives

Areas of open water

Frogs and toads are slug-eating allies

Shallow water

Water for wildlife
A garden pond is beneficial for wildlife and should entice some great slug-eating allies, the frogs and toads.

FLASHLIGHT SLUG HUNTING

Perhaps you can be the natural predator—armed with just a few slug-hunting accessories.

Why slug hunt?

Hand-removal is often recommended as a counter-slug strategy, either by searching under pots and other hidey-holes during the day or by a nighttime search. However, there's a lack of scientific evidence for this labor-intensive method.

Despite the lack of studies, a nocturnal garden tour is worth trying. It gives you the chance to see the slugs that are currently feeding on your plants. Compared to many other methods, such as daytime hunts, beer traps (see pp128–29), and nematodes (see p130), there's little risk of accidentally targeting the other slugs that are neutral or beneficial in the garden.

How to slug hunt

Year-round and night-long slug hunting is unlikely to be productive. Slugs are most active in mild, damp weather and cause the most harm to seedlings and soft lettuces, so focus on spring, early summer, and fall.

Armed with a good flashlight, preferably a head lamp for hands-free, and a container for the slug collecting, you can head out to inspect your plants. You might want gloves or a spoon to scoop the slugs. Bare hands can be more dexterous, but remember to wash them well afterward (see p46).

When to slug hunt

As to the time of night, as we've seen, different species have different peaks of activity (see p26), but the biggest plant nibbler, the gray field slug (see p88), is active just after sunset. Some recommendations from gardening authors include:

- Three or four consecutive evenings every two weeks in warmer weather
- Every evening after planting and every other night from early May to the end of June
- Regular flashlight patrols two to three hours after sunset

Nighttime hunt
A nighttime slug hunt gives you a chance to see which slugs are active in your garden and relocate the ones that are munching on your plants.

- When sensitive plants are emerging from the ground, daily on damp spring evenings.

What to do with the slugs?
I prefer the most slug-friendly option of relocating the slugs in your garden, such as to the compost heap or a patch with dense vegetation. That way, they can live on and continue their role in the garden ecosystem. However, they may roam, and some species have homing instincts, so this strategy will need to tolerate the chance of them returning.

I no longer recommend relocating to a field or open area because non-native species are increasing in gardens, and we should avoid introducing them into habitats where they might currently be absent.

If you're unwilling to let them live to slug another day, the most humane way to dispatch a slug is to drown it in 5 percent alcohol (such as beer) or carbonated water, which both have an anaesthetic effect. Killing with salt is not a gentle death, and while putting slugs on a bird feeder might return them to the food chain, it could instead lead to a slow, sun-baked demise.

SHELTER AND BEER TRAPS

If you aren't able, or willing, to hunt slugs at nighttime, perhaps you can get them to come to you. There are various scientific studies on trapping methods, but these are used to monitor slug populations throughout the year, usually for farmers to time the application of slug pellets to fields. For that reason, they don't necessarily tell us whether plants can be protected using traps.

Shelter traps
Providing a slug refuge lets you see what numbers and species are active. This can be fun if you are setting out on a slug-identification mission (see pp44–45). But if you want to manage slugs, you will need to follow up with a way of relocating or disposing of them (see p127).

Trap materials you could try include roofing shingles, weathered bricks, ceramic tile, inverted plant pot saucers, wooden boards, or cardboard squares. The latter three were tested by RHS student Imogen Cavadino at RHS Garden Wisley, and they caught similar numbers of slugs, more when placed in beds rather than on the lawn. The catch could be greatly increased by adding a bait of bran mash, although this sped up the disintegration of the cardboard trap or it being taken by foxes or badgers.

These traps are more likely to catch larger slugs than smaller species or juveniles. Again, this makes them useful for ID practice, but less so for slug management. It's best to check your trap early in the morning because the slugs are likely to vacate if it is too sunny.

Beer traps
Beer traps are a topic that many people get excited about, perhaps because you can see and count the grisly result of your efforts! They usually consist of a container of beer

Providing a slug refuge lets you see what numbers and species are active.

BEER TRAP **SHELTER TRAP**

Traps
Beer and shelter traps may catch slugs,
but the jury's still out on whether they
protect nearby plants.

sunk into the soil, often covered with a lid. There are commercially produced trap structures available, but it is unlikely that these are superior to a homemade version.

There have been several studies testing what types of beer catch the most slugs. One study by Cranshaw found that fermented aromas seem more essential than alcohol content, with non-alcoholic malted beverages and water with sugar or yeast catching as many or more slugs than beer. This study also found that the type of yeast made a difference, with lager yeast being more attractive than

baking or ale yeast. However, there is almost no evidence for whether these traps reduce plant damage in the vicinity.

One study by Dankowska found that increasing trap catches were related to decreasing plant damage, but the study was over a single large area with multiple types of traps (beer and pesticide) present.

Another major drawback to beer traps is that you may attract all kinds of slug friends as well as foes. Ground beetles, which are slug predators, and other wildlife might also be unlucky enough to fall in.

BIOLOGICAL CONTROLS

Like natural predators, biological control agents exploit the natural food web to help keep slugs in check. This usually involves bringing in predators or parasites and applying them en masse, so care should be taken to avoid unintended effects.

Nematodes

Nematodes are microscopic, wormlike organisms, and are a hugely diverse group including plant parasites, animal parasites, and free-living species. Although there are many species of gastropod-parasitic nematodes, only one has been widely used for biological control of slugs over the last 30 years—*Phasmarhabditis hermaphrodita*.

Phasmarhabditis nematodes are naturally occurring in the soil in many parts of the world, but *P. hermaphrodita* is most likely native to Europe. They enter slugs' bodies and reproduce in the mantle, leaving the slug swollen and eventually dead. They further reproduce in the corpse before dispersing into the soil to find another host.

These nematodes can infect most species of slugs, although some are more susceptible than others, especially juveniles and the smaller species, including the gray field slug (see p88). They are effective against the long-keeled slugs that are often responsible for holey potatoes, and because they are hidden underground, they provide one of the few ways to protect potatoes.

This nematode biocontrol is available to purchase in Europe but is not currently available in the US or elsewhere, although there is ongoing research into similar species around the world, including in North America.

Future biocontrol

Sciomyzid flies (see p41) hold potential as a future biological control. It is an eco-friendly if not slug-friendly method because, compared to nematodes, the flies are rather more specific about which host gastropods they will parasitize. They are harder to rear in captivity and are likely to be hard to "apply" in the field, but research is ongoing.

It might be possible to breed and release ground beetles (see pp40, 125) in enclosed areas like greenhouses. However, it is not a good idea to release them more widely because they are more generalist predators and might have unintended impacts. Progress on this front is more likely to center on effective ways to support wild populations of beetles.

ABOVE The swollen mantle of this gray field slug shows it's been parasitized by *Phasmarhabditis* nematodes.

RIGHT *Phasmarhabditis hermaphrodita* nematodes can infect most species of slugs.

PROTECTING VULNERABLE PLANTS

Do you desperately want to grow hostas, strawberries, or lettuce, but your patch is a slug haven? You will need to strategize.

Integrated Gastropod Management
Many gardeners already tend to instinctively adopt the principles of Integrated Pest Management (IPM; see pp107, 108). But to get a really good harvest or display of plants that are slug favorites, you will need to *embrace* IPM, or, in this case, Integrated Gastropod Management.

This means taking a holistic view of your plot and combining a range of the tools and methods that have been outlined in this chapter.
Cultural controls Have you planted your garden with diversity in mind or do you have hedgerows, long grass, and nettle patches around the edge of your garden? If not, can you add any wilder patches or other slug predator habitats?
Plant husbandry Are there slug-resistant plant varieties available? Can you grow your seedlings on a bench or your plants in pots raised off the ground? Once in the ground, have you added a good mulch and set your alarm early for a strict morning watering regimen (see p113)?
Construct defenses Have you tried some of the deterrents discussed on pp114–21? A cloche for very small plants in the ground might slow the overground travel of the large *Arion* slugs, but they may, of course, dig underneath and pop up inside.
On the prowl What's the most vulnerable part of the plant season—budding, seedling, or fruiting? Head out in the evenings with your head lamp and container to grab and relocate the slugs as they home in on the tender delicacies (see pp126–27).

If this array of cultural and physical measures is not enough to reduce plant feeding to a tolerable level, you might want to resort to more slug-lethal options, such as nematode biological control, which is only available in Europe (see p130).

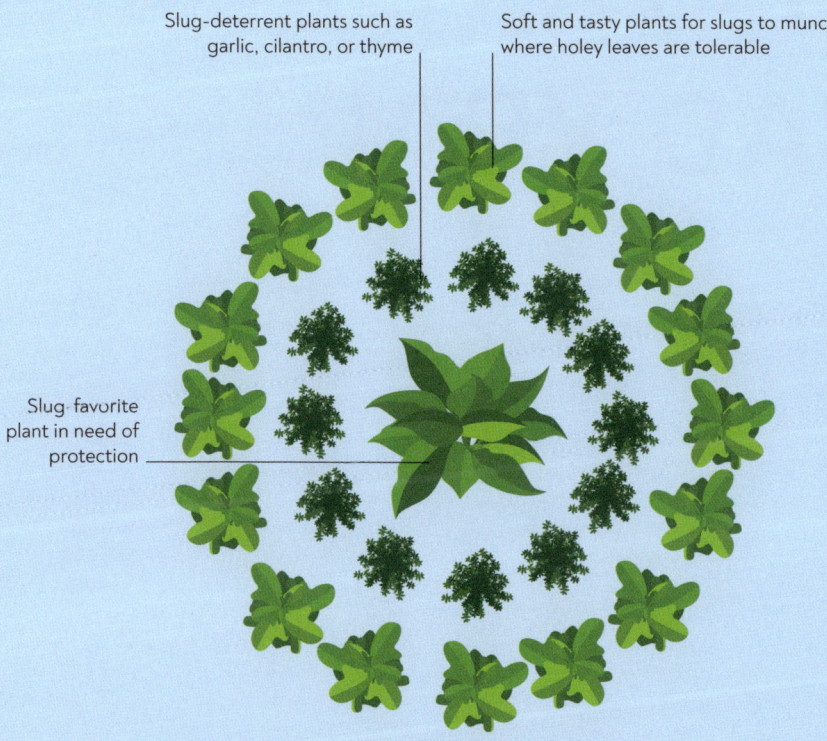

Slug-deterrent plants such as garlic, cilantro, or thyme

Soft and tasty plants for slugs to munch, where holey leaves are tolerable

Slug-favorite plant in need of protection

Push-pull strategy
No proven plant combinations exist, but you can incorporate push-pull techniques to create fortifications around your prized plants.

Push-pull strategy

The push-pull strategy involves adding slug deterrents among the plants to be protected, and a slug attractant nearby to tempt them away.

One published example of this targeted invasive snails in Australia. Garlic powder was successfully used as the deterrent, and red posts were installed as the attractant, as these snails like to roost in elevated places.

No proven push-pull strategies have been developed for slugs yet, but this is definitely food for thought. You may be able to trial your own, perhaps using a variety of deterrents and some sacrificial lettuce to tempt slugs.

COMBAT A BAD YEAR

When damp and drizzle persist and slugs are thriving, what can you do to save your beloved plants?

Know your foe

In 2024, the UK weather was ideal for slugs—a mild winter followed by a long, damp spring and minimal dry periods in the summer. These perfect slug conditions meant they flourished. The RHS Gardening Advice service had plenty of inquiries on the topic, and it became the sluggiest year on record.

We can never reliably predict what the season ahead will bring, but a mild winter is always a good hint that a sluggy spring may be incoming, which can help you prepare. Use the management techniques that are informed by science outlined in this chapter to help protect your plants.

Focus your efforts

Recent research using high-tech slug-tagging techniques (in fields) has shown how slug distribution is patchy, and that slugs tend to stick to these patches, providing lots of potential for targeted management. Gardeners can be even more focused than farmers by knowing which plants are most sensitive and concentrating protective efforts on those, while being more relaxed in other areas.

Plan for the future

Climate change looms, with widespread implications for slugs and their ecosystems. Impacts will vary by species, but the gray field slug (see p88) is expected to become more numerous in areas that will become warm but remain damp, such as northwest Scotland, and scarcer where the trend is for warmer and drier conditions, such as southwest England.

As one of the many impacts of climate change, this means gardeners and growers of all kinds will need to be adaptable and adopt the findings of ongoing research for

their plant choices, water management techniques, and timing of seasonal activities.

Embrace your friends

The best way to cope with slugs is to learn to live with them! Feeling frustrated and even heartbroken at the destruction of your favorite plants or new seedlings is understandable, but slugs aren't monsters. As we now know, many slug species aren't even feeding on plants but instead helpfully recycling, and all have a role to play in the garden ecosystem.

In a philosophical study of gardeners' attitudes to slugs, Ginn found a frequent "combination of killing slugs but professing guilt." This is a view I encounter a lot, with only a memorable few demonstrating remorseless slug slaughter. I expect, however, that attitudes will continue to shift toward tolerant frustration and prioritizing of biodiversity.

I hope that this book has helped you to feel friendlier toward slugs. Even if it hasn't made you love their slimy, tentacled little faces, I hope to leave you with at least an appreciation for these biologically fascinating and admirably efficient omnivorous garden creatures.

BIBLIOGRAPHY

Introduction
8 Rowson, B. et al., *Slugs of Britain and Ireland: Identification, Understanding and Control*, Field Studies Council, 2014a.
10 Breure, B. & Heer, S. de "From a 'domestic commodity' to a 'secret of trade': snails and shells of land molluscs in early (mainly 16th and 17th century) visual arts", *Basteria*, 79, pp81–97, 2015 · Grandville, J.J., illustrations from *The Flowers Personified*, *The Public Domain Review*, 1847, publicdomainreview.org/collection/the-flowers-personified-1847/
11 BBC News, "Artist Monster Chetwynd's Giant Slugs 'Slime' Tate Britain", bbc.com/news/entertainment-arts-46399187 · UCSC, "Our Mascot: Sammy the Banana Slug – UC Santa Cruz", ucsc.edu/campus/mascot/ · Bartsch, P., "Our poison gas detector and how it was discovered", *Journal of the Washington Academy of Sciences*, 10 (10), p309, 1920 · Svanberg, I., "Black slugs (*Arion ater*) as grease: A case study of technical use of gastropods in pre-industrial Sweden", *Journal of Ethnobiology*, 26 (2), pp299–309, 2006.

What are gastropods?
14 South, A., *Terrestrial Slugs: Biology, Ecology and Control*, 2nd edn, Chapman & Hall, 1992 · Cameron, R., *Slugs and Snails*, Collins New Naturalist Library, book 133, HarperCollins, 2016.
15 Rowson et al. 2014a.
16 South 1992 · Gómez, B.J., "Structure and functioning of the reproductive system", in *The Biology of Terrestrial Molluscs*, G. Barker (ed.), pp307–30, CABI Publishing, 2001 · Rowson et al. 2014a.
17 Illustration adapted from Wiktor, A., "Agriolimacidae (Gastropoda: Pulmonata) – a systematic monograph", *Annales Zoologici*, 49 (4), p374, 2000.
18 Cameron 2016 · Wiktor 2000 · Rowson et al. 2014a.
20 Rowson et al. 2014a · Rowson, B. et al., "The slugs of Britain and Ireland: Undetected and undescribed species increase a well-studied, economically important fauna by more than 20%", *PLOS ONE*, 9 (4), pe91907, 2014b, doi.org/10.1371/journal.pone.0091907 · Anderson, R. & Rowson, B., "An annotated list of the non-marine molluscs of Britain and Ireland", *Journal of Conchology*, 2020 · MolluscaBase, *Number of records in MolluscaBase*,

2024 molluscabase.org/aphia.php?p=stats Nekola (2014) Overview of the North American Terrestrial Gastropod Fauna. *American Malacological Bulletin 32*: 225-235. https://doi.org/10.4003/006.032.0203
21 Rowson et al. 2014a · Cameron, R., "Speedy snails (and speedier slugs)", *Mollusc World | The Conchological Society of Great Britain and Ireland*, 36, pp3–4, 2014.
22 White-McLean, J.A., *Ariolimax columbianus, Terrestrial Mollusk Tool. USDA APHIS PPQ S&T Identification Technology Program and the University of Florida*, 2011, idtools.org/mollusk/index.cfm?packageID=1178&entity ID=8185 · Department of Climate Change, Energy, the Environment and Water, Canberra, "Social media technology could save our slug!", 2023, dcceew.gov.au/about/news/digital-stories/social-media-technology-could-save-our-slug
23 Cameron 2016 · Barker, G.M. (ed.) *Molluscs as Crop Pests*, CABI Publishing, 2002 · Mc Donnell, R. et al., *Slugs: A Guide to the Invasive and Native Fauna of California*, UCANR Publications, 2024 · Murphy, M., "The IUCN Red List of threatened species: *Triboniophorus* sp. nov. 'Kaputar'", *IUCN Red List of Threatened Species*, 2014, iucnredlist.org/en · Byrne, A. et al., "Irish Red List No. 2 – Non-marine molluscs", National Parks and Wildlife Service, Dublin, 2009 · Neubert, E. et al., *European Red List of terrestrial molluscs: snails, slugs, and semi-slugs*, 2019, portals.iucn.org/library/node/48439 · Willis, J.C. et al., "Use of an individual-based model to forecast the effect of climate change on the dynamics, abundance and geographical range of the pest slug *Deroceras reticulatum* in the UK", *Global Change Biology*, 12 (9), pp1643–57, 2006.

Your garden ecosystem
26 South 1992.
28 Barnes, H.F. & Weil, J.W. "Slugs in gardens: Their numbers, activities and distribution. Part 2", *Journal of Animal Ecology*, 14 (2), pp71–105, 1945.
29 Weber, D. et al., "Climate change alters slug abundance but not herbivory in a temperate grassland", *PLOS ONE*, 18 (3), pe0283128, 2023.
30 Denny, M.W. & Gosline, J.M., "The

physical properties of the pedal mucus of the terrestrial slug, *Ariolimax columbianus*", *Journal of Experimental Biology*, 88 (1), pp375–94, 1980 · Li, J. et al., "Tough adhesives for diverse wet surfaces", *Science*, 357 (6349), pp378–81, 2017 · Luchtel, D.L. & Deyrup-Olsen, I. "Body wall: form and function", in Barker 2001.
32 Cameron 2016 · Cook, A., "Behavioural ecology: On doing the right thing, in the right place at the right time", in Barker 2001 · Henderson, I. & Triebskorn, R. "Chemical control of terrestrial gastropods", in Barker 2002.
34, 36, 38 South 1992.
36 Dirzo, R., "Experimental studies on slug-plant interactions: I. The acceptability of thirty plant species to the slug *Agriolimax caruaneae*", *The Journal of Ecology*, pp981–98, 1980 · Moles, A.T. et al., "Correlations between physical and chemical defences in plants: tradeoffs, syndromes, or just many different ways to skin a herbivorous cat?", *New Phytologist*, 198 (1), pp252–63, 2013 · Buschmann, H. et al., "The effect of slug grazing on vegetation development and plant species diversity in an experimental grassland", *Functional Ecology*, 19 (2), pp291–98, 2005 · Allan, E. & Crawley, M.J., "Contrasting effects of insect and molluscan herbivores on plant diversity in a long-term field experiment", *Ecology Letters*, 14 (12), pp1246–53, 2011.
38 Allen, J.A., "Avian and mammalian predators of terrestrial gastropods", in *Natural Enemies of Terrestrial Molluscs*, CABI Publishing, pp1–36, 2004 · Cleary, G.P. et al., "The diet of the badger *Meles meles* in the Republic of Ireland", *Mammalian Biology*, 74, pp438–47, 2009. · Carnegie Museum of Natural History (https://carnegiemnh.org/mollusks/)
40 Dearborn et al. 2014. (https://bioone.org/journals/the-coleopterists-bulletin/volume-68/issue-3/072.068.0317/The-Ground-Beetle-Coleoptera-Carabidae-Fauna-of-Maine-USA/10.1649/072.068.0317.full). Symondson, W.O. "Coleoptera (Carabidae, Staphylinidae, Lampyridae, Drilidae and Silphidae) as predators of terrestrial gastropods", in *Natural Enemies of Terrestrial Molluscs*, CABI Publishing, 2004 · Bohan, D.A. et al. "Spatial dynamics of predation by carabid

beetles on slugs", *Journal of Animal Ecology*, 69 (3), pp367–79, 2000, doi. org/10.1046/j.1365-2656.2000.00399.x • Barua, A. et al., "A literature review of biological and bio-rational control strategies for slugs: Current research and future prospects", *Insects*, 12 (6), p541, 2021 • Pakarinen, E. "The importance of mucus as a defence against carabid beetles by the slugs *Arion fasciatus* and *Deroceras reticulatum*", *Journal of Molluscan Studies*, 60 (2), pp149–55, 1994 • UKBeetles *Lampyris noctiluca*, ukbeetles.co.uk/lampyris-noctiluca • Gardiner, T. & Didham, R.K., "Glowing, glowing, gone? Monitoring long-term trends in glow-worm numbers in south-east England", *Insect Conservation and Diversity*, 13 (2), pp162–74, 2020.
41 Murphy, W.L. et al., "Key aspects of the biology of snail-killing Sciomyzidae flies", *Annual Review of Entomology*, 57, pp425–47, 2012 • Barker, G. et al. "Overview of the biology of marsh flies (Diptera: Sciomyzidae), with special reference to predators and parasitoids of terrestrial gastropods", in *Natural Enemies of Terrestrial Molluscs*, CABI Publishing, 2004 • Barker, G.M., "Millipedes (Diplopoda) and centipedes (Chilopoda) (Myriapoda) as predators of terrestrial gastropods", in *Natural Enemies of Terrestrial Molluscs*, CABI Publishing, pp405–25, 2004.

Friend or foe?

44 Eversham, B., "Identifying British Slugs", Wildlife Trust for Bedfordshire, Cambridgeshire, Northamptonshire, 2018, wildlifebcn.org/sites/default/files/2018-06 /Identifying%20British%20Slugs%20v%20 3.1%20%20iv2018_0.pdf • Rowson et al. 2014a • Cavadino, I. et al., "Slugs Count: Assessing citizen scientist engagement and development, and the accuracy of their identifications", *People and Nature*, 6 (5), pp1822–37, 2024.
46 Fischer, K. (2023) *What Is Rat Lungworm?*, WebMD, 2023, webmd. com/a-to-z-guides/what-is-rat-lungworm • Paredes-Esquivel, C. et al., "Neuroangiostrongyliasis: Rat lungworm invades Europe", *The American Journal of Tropical Medicine and Hygiene*, 108 (4), p857, 2023.
53 Wiktor 2000.
55–100 Rowson et al. 2014a.
58 Zajac, K. et al., "*Arion vulgaris*

Moquin-Tandon, 1855 – the aetiology of an invasive species", *Folia Malacologica*, 25 (2), 2017 • Delivering Alien Invasive Species Inventories for Europe (DAISIE), *Handbook of Alien Species in Europe*, Springer Netherlands, 2008, books. google.co.uk/books?id=_g-syyoXw2gC • Slotsbo, S., "Ecophysiology and life history of the slug *Arion lusitanicus*", PhD thesis, Aarhus Universitet, Institut for Agroøkologi, 2021 • Davies, S.M., "*Arion flagellus* (Collinge) and *A. lusitanicus* (Mabille) in the British Isles: A morphological, biological and taxonomic investigation", *Journal of Conchology*, 32 (6), pp339–54, 1987.
60 Quinteiro, J. et al., "Phylogeny of slug species of the genus *Arion*: Evidence of monophyly of Iberian endemics and of the existence of relict species in Pyrenean refuges", *Journal of Zoological Systematics and Evolutionary Research*, 43 (2), pp139–48, 2005 • Cavadino, I., "Garden gastropods: Using citizen science to understand the diversity, role and impact of slug and snail species in British gardens", PhD thesis, Newcastle University, 2023.
62 Zemanova, M.A. et al., "Slimy invasion: Climatic niche and current and future biogeography of *Arion* slug invaders", *Diversity and Distributions*, 24 (11), pp1627–40, 2018 • Mc Donnell et al. 2024 • Keane, R.M. & Crawley, M.J., "Exotic plant invasions and the enemy release hypothesis", *Trends in Ecology & Evolution*, 17 (4), pp164–70, 2002.
64 Port, G. & Ester, A., "Gastropods as pests in vegetable and ornamental crops in Western Europe", in Barker 2002, pp337–51 • Mc Donnell et al. 2024.
66 Anderson, R., "*Arion owenii*, Inishowen slug S.M. Davies, 1979", MolluscIreland: Land and Freshwater Molluscs, 2024, habitas.org.uk/molluscireland/species. php?item=34
68 Jordaens, K. et al., "Mixed breeding system in the hermaphroditic land slug *Arion intermedius* (Stylommatophora, Arionidae)", *Hereditas*, 150 (4–6), pp45–52, 2013.
70 Byrne et al. 2009.
72 National Biodiversity Network (NBN), *Species search/NBN Atlas*, 2024 species, nbnatlas.org/species • Symondson, W.O.C., "Does *Tandonia budapestensis* (Mollusca: Pulmonata) contain toxins? Evidence from feeding trials with the

slug predator *Pterostichus melanarius* (Coleoptera: Carabidae)", *Journal of Molluscan Studies*, 63 (4), pp541–45, 1997.
74 Clemente, N.L. et al., "Biology and individual growth of *Milax gagates* (Draparnaud, 1801) (Pulmonata: Stylommatophora)", *Invertebrate Reproduction & Development*, 54 (3), pp163–68, 2010.
78 Quick, H.E., "British slugs (Pulmonata; Testacellidae, Arionidae, Limacidae)", *Bulletin of the British Museum (Natural History) Zoology*, pp103–226, 1960.
80 Lister, M., plate 101b, in *Historiae sive Synopsis Methodicae Conchyliorum quorum Omnium Picturae, ad vivum delineate, exhibetur. Liber Primus, qui est de Cochleis Terrestribus*, London, 1685 • Davis, M.A. et al., "Don't judge species on their origins", *Nature*, 474 (7350), pp153–54, 2011.
82 Cavadino 2023 • Rowson et al. 2014b • Cook, A., "Huddling and the control of water loss by the slug *Limax pseudoflavus* Evans", *Animal Behaviour*, 29 (1), pp289–98, 1981.
84 du Feu, C., "Field ID of Slugs", Field Studies Council, 2017.
86 Hutchinson, J.M.C. et al., "Will the real *Limax nyctelius* please step forward: *Lehmannia*, *Ambigolimax*, or *Malacolimax*? No, *Letourneuxia*! msrevacc:2022-05-03", *Archiv für Molluskenkunde International Journal of Malacology*, 151 (1), pp19–41, 2022 • Quick 1960.
88 Howlett, S.A., "The biology, behaviour and control of the field slug, *Deroceras reticulatum* (Müller)", PhD thesis, Newcastle University, 2005 • AHDB, *What are the main slug species of UK crops?* ahdb.org.uk/knowledge-library/ what-are-the-main-slug-species-of-uk-crops • Barker 2002.
90 Hutchinson, J., Reise, H. & Robinson, D., "A biography of an invasive terrestrial slug: The spread, distribution and habitat of *Deroceras invadens*", *NeoBiota*, 23, pp17–64, 2014.
92 Welter-Schultes, F., *European Non-marine Molluscs, a Guide for Species Identification*, Planet Poster Editions, 2012 • South 1992 • Quick 1960. McDonnell et al., *Slugs: A Guide to the Introduced and Native Fauna of California* (2024).
94 Gunn, A., "The ecology of the introduced slug *Boettgerilla pallens* (Simroth) in North Wales", *Journal of*

Molluscan Studies, 58 (4), pp449–53, 1992 · Reise, H. et al., "The ecology and rapid spread of the terrestrial slug *Boettgerilla pallens* in Europe with reference to its recent discovery in North America", *The Veliger*, 43 (4), pp313–18, 2000.
96 Rowson, B. & Symondson, W.O.C. "*Selenochlamys ysbryda* sp. nov. from Wales, UK: A *Testacella*-like slug new to western Europe (Stylommatophora: Trigonochlamydidae)", *Journal of Conchology*, 39 (5), 2008.
98 Turbanov, I. & Balashov, I., "A second record of *Selenochlamys* (Stylommatophora: Trigonochlamydidae) from Crimea", *Malacologica Bohemoslovaca*, 14, pp1–4, 2015 · Rowson & Symondson 2008.
100 Cameron, R., *Land Snails in the British Isles AIDGAP*, Field Studies Council, 2003 · Forsyth, R.G. (2004) *Land Snails of British Columbia*, Royal BC Museum Handbook.

What can gardeners do?
104 Hill, T., *The Profitable Arte of Gardening*, Henrie Bynneman, 1568 · South 1992.
105 Barker 2002.
106 Bailey, S.E.R., "Molluscicidal baits for control of terrestrial gastropods", in Barker 2002 · Howlett, S.A., "Terrestrial slug problems: Classical biological control and beyond", *CABI Reviews*, pp1–10, 2012 · Perry, L. et al., "National toxicovigilance for pesticide exposures resulting in health care contact – An example from the UK's National Poisons Information Service", *Clinical Toxicology*, 52 (5), pp549–55, 2014 · Bertero, A. et al., "Types of pesticides involved in domestic and wild animal poisoning in Italy", *Science of The Total Environment*, 707, 136129, 2020 · Castle, G.D. et al., "Review of the molluscicide metaldehyde in the environment", *Environmental Science: Water Research & Technology*. 3 (3), pp415–28, 2017 · GOV.UK, "Outdoor use of metaldehyde to be banned to protect wildlife", 2020, gov.uk/government/news/outdoor-use-of-metaldehyde-to-be-banned-to-protect-wildlife · Edwards, C.A. et al., "The relative toxicity of metaldehyde and iron phosphate-based molluscicides to earthworms", *Crop Protection*, 28 (4), pp289–94, 2009 · Chemicals Regulation Division, "Amateur product labelling – Efficacy aspects", 2017, hse.gov.uk/pesticides/resources/G/g212.pdf · Lewis, K.A. et al., "An international database for pesticide risk assessments and management", *Human and Ecological Risk Assessment: An International Journal*, 22 (4), pp1050–64,

2016 · Metaldehyde report, sitem.herts.ac.uk/aeru/ppdb/en/Reports/446.htm · Food and Agriculture Organization of the United Nations, "Integrated Pest Management (IPM)", fao.org/pest-and-pesticide-management/ipm/integrated-pest-management/en/ · Health and Safety Executive, *Amateur Pesticide User Habits Survey 2019*, hse.gov.uk/pesticides/assets/docs/Garden_User_Habits_Survey_Report_2019.pdf
107 Office for National Statistics, *UK Natural Capital: Urban Accounts, 2019*, ons.gov.uk/economy/environmentalaccounts/bulletins/uknaturalcapital/urbanaccounts#toc
109 Dirzo 1980 · Bowdens Nursery, "2024 Catalogue", bowdensnursery.com/categories/2024-Catalogue/ · South 1992.
110 Certis Belchim UK, "Slugwatch forecast" certisbelchim.co.uk/crop-focus/slugs/slugwatch-forecast/ · South 1992 · Runham, N.W. & Hunter, P.J., *Terrestrial Slugs*, Hutchinson University Library, 1970.
111 Agriculture and Horticulture Development Board, "Factsheet: Integrated slug control", 2020 · Cook, R.T. et al., "The potential for common weeds to reduce slug damage to winter wheat: Laboratory and fields studies", *Journal of Applied Ecology*, 34 (1), pp79–87, 1997 · Bianchi, F.J.J.A. et al., "Sustainable pest regulation in agricultural landscapes: a review on landscape composition, biodiversity and natural pest control", *Proceedings of the Royal Society B: Biological Sciences*, 273 (1595), pp1715–27, 2006.
112 South 1992 · Runham & Hunter 1970 · Glen, D., "Integrated control of slug damage in organic vegetable crops", DEFRA project OF0158, 2002.
113 Speiser, B. & Hochstrasser, M., "Slug damage in relation to watering regime", *Agriculture, Ecosystems & Environment*, 70 (2), pp273–75, 1998 · Schüder, I. et al. "Barriers, repellents and antifeedants for slug and snail control", *Crop Protection*, 22 (8), pp1033–38, 2003 · Schüder. I. et al., "The behavioural response of slugs and snails to novel molluscicides, irritants and repellents", *Pest Management Science*, 60 (12), pp1171–77, 2004.
117 Thompson, J.M. et al., "Effect of copper hydroxide on slug feeding", *Journal of Environmental Horticulture*, 23 (4), pp167–70, 2005 · Capinera, J.L. & Dickens, K., "Some effects of copper-based fungicides on plant-feeding terrestrial molluscs: A role for repellents in mollusc management", *Crop Protection*, 83, pp76–82, 2016 · Hoyer, S.A. & Myrick, C.A., "Can copper-based

substrates be used to protect hatcheries from invasion by the New Zealand mudsnail?", *North American Journal of Aquaculture*, 74 (4), pp575–83, 2012 · Schüder, I. et al. 2003 · Watz, J. & Nyqvist, D., "Artificial barriers against arionid slug movement", *Crop Protection*, 142, 105525, 2021 · Henderson, I. and Triebskorn, R., "Chemical control of terrestrial gastropods", in Barker 2022, pp1–31 · Köhler, H.-R. et al., "Expression of the stress-70 protein family (HSP70) due to heavy metal contamination in the slug, *Deroceras reticulatum*: An approach to monitor sublethal stress conditions", *Chemosphere*, 33 (7), pp1327–40, 1996 · Hall, A.H., "Eradication of slugs and snails", *Nature*, 130 (3274), p170, 1932.
118 Hollingsworth, R.G. et al., "Caffeine as a repellent for slugs and snails", *Nature*, 417 (6892), pp915–16, 2002 · Horgan, F.G. et al., "Spent coffee grounds applied as a top-dressing or incorporated into the soil can improve plant growth while reducing slug herbivory", *Agriculture*, 13 (2), p257, 2023 · Lewis, K.A. et al., "An international database for pesticide risk assessments and management", *Human and Ecological Risk Assessment: An International Journal*, 22 (4), pp1050–64, 2016 · Caffeine report, sitem.herts.ac.uk/aeru/ppdb/en/Reports/3651.htm · Capinera, J.L., "Assessment of barrier materials to protect plants from Florida leatherleaf slug (Mollusca: Gastropoda: Veronicellidae)", *Florida Entomologist*, 101 (3), pp373–81, 2018 · Watz & Nyqvist 2021 · Zeni, V. et al., "Diatomaceous earth for arthropod pest control: Back to the future", *Molecules*, 26 (24), p7487, 2021.
119 "Organic slug and snail controls", *Which? Gardening*, pp16–19, April 2023 · Schüder et al. 2003 · Laznik, Ž. et al., "Contact efficacy of different wood ashes against Spanish slug, *Arion vulgaris* (Gastropoda: Arionidae)", *Applied Sciences*, 10 (23), p8564, 2020 · Evans, A. et al., "Row covers: Effects of wool and other materials on pest numbers, microclimate, and crop quality", *Journal of Economic Entomology*, 90 (6), pp1661–64, 1997 · Laznik, Ž. & Trdan, S., "Is a combination of different natural substances suitable for slug (*Arion* spp.) control?", *Spanish Journal of Agricultural Research*, 14(3), p20, 2016 · Glen 2002.
120 Schüder et al. 2003 · Barua et al. 2021 · Health and Safety Executive, "Garden home – information and advice to those using pesticides in their garden, allotment, or on their houseplants", 2020, hse.gov.uk/pesticides/user-areas/

garden-home.htm · Dodds, C.J. et al., "Action of extracts of Apiaceae on feeding behavior and neurophysiology of the field slug *Deroceras reticulatum*", *Journal of Chemical Ecology*, 25 (9), pp2127–45, 1999 · Glen 2002 · Klein, M.L. et al. "Acute toxicity of essential oils to the pest slug *Deroceras reticulatum* in laboratory and greenhouse bioassays", *Journal of Pest Science*, 93 (1), pp415–25, 2020 · Griffin, M. et al., "Silicon reduces slug feeding on wheat seedlings", *Journal of Pest Science*, 88 (1), pp17–24, 2015 · Mortensen, B., "Plant resistance against herbivory", *Nature Education Knowledge*, 4 (4), 2013 · McDonald-Howard, K. et al., "An investigation into the combination of the parasitic nematode *Phasmarhabditis hermaphroditu* and cedarwood oil to control pestiferous slugs", *Crop Protection*, 179, 106601, 2024.

122 British Trust for Ornithology (BTO), "Putting up nest boxes for birds", bto.org/how-you-can-help/providing-birds/putting-nest-boxes-birds · Garden Wildlife Health (GWH) "Feeding garden birds best practice guidance", 2021, gardenwildlifehealth.org/garden-wildlife/ · RSPB, "How and when to feed birds in your garden", rspb.org.uk/birds-and-wildlife/helping-birds-and-wildlife

123 Bosshardt, S. et al., "Changing perspectives on chicken-pastured orchards for action: A review based on a heuristic model", *Agricultural Systems*, 196, 103335, 2022.

124 Baker, J. et al., *Amphibian Habitat Management Handbook*, Amphibian and Reptile Conservation, 2011 · Symondson, W.O.C. et al., "Dynamics of the relationship between a generalist predator and slugs over five years", *Ecology*, 83 (1), pp137–47, 2002.

125 Edgar, P. et al., *Reptile Habitat Management Handbook*, Amphibian and Reptile Conservation, 2010 · Fusser, M.S. et al. "Effects of landscape composition on carabids and slugs in herbaceous and woody field margins", *Agriculture, Ecosystems & Environment*, 226, pp79–87, 2016 · Kromp, B., "Carabid beetles in sustainable agriculture: A review on pest control efficacy, cultivation impacts and enhancement", *Agriculture, Ecosystems & Environment*, 74, pp187–228, 1999 · Jowett, K. et al., "Species matter when considering landscape effects on carabid distributions", *Agriculture, Ecosystems & Environment*, 285, 106631, 2019.

126 Abercrombie, J., *Abercrombie's Practical Gardener*, T. Cadell & W. Davies, 1817 · McKee, A. & Gatter, M.,

The Polytunnel Handbook, Green Books, 2008 · Buczacki, S.T. & Harris, K.M., *Pests, Diseases and Disorders of Garden Plants*, 4th edn, Collins, 2014 · Bird, S.K., personal communication, 2024.

127 South 1992 · Rowson et al. 2014b · Cavadino 2023 · Fossati, P. et al., "Welfare of invertebrates: A pilot study on a new land snail stunning technique", *Scientific Reports*, 14 (1), p8378, 2024 · Gilbertson, C.R. & Wyatt, J.D., "Evaluation of euthanasia techniques for an invertebrate species, land snails (*Succinea putris*)", *Journal of the American Association for Laboratory Animal Science*, 55 (5), p577, 2016.

128 Cavadino 2023 · Glen, D. et al., "Further development of farmer-friendly methods for estimating slug infestation incidence in soil and damage risk to oilseed rape", *Final Project Report* (preprint), 2004 ufop.de/files/9013/3922/7287/FurthrFarmerFriendly.pdf · Schrim, M. & Byers, R.A., "A method for sampling three slug species attacking sod-seeded legumes (*Deroceras reticulatum, Deroceras laeve*)", *Melsheimer Entomological Series* (preprint), 1980.

129 Hagnell, J. et al., "How to trap a slug: Commercial versus homemade slug traps", *Crop Protection*, 25 (3), pp212–15, 2006 · Smith, F.F. & Boswell, A.L., "New baits and attractants for slugs", *Journal of Economic Entomology*, 63 (6), pp1919–22, 1970 · Piechowicz, B. et al., "Beer as olfactory attractant in the fight against harmful slugs *Arion lusitanicus* Mabille 1868", *Chemistry-Didactics-Ecology-Metrology*, 19 (1–2), pp119–25, 2014 · Cranshaw, W., "Attractiveness of beer and fermentation products to the gray garden slug, *Agriolimax reticulatum* (Muller) (Mollusca: Limacidae)", *Technical Bulletin TB97-1*, Colorado Agricultural Experiment Station, 1997 · Dankowska, E., "Effectiveness of beer traps and molluscicides as means of gastropod control", *Folia Malacologica*, 19 (4), pp273–75, 2011.

130 R. Rae et al., "Thirty years of slug control using the parasitic nematode and beyond", *Pest Management Science*, 79 (10), pp3408–24, 2023 · Wilson et al., "The rhabditid nematode *Phasmarhabditis hermaphrodita* as a potential biological control agent for slugs", *Biocontrol Science and Technology*, 3 (4), pp503–11, 1993 · Barua et al. 2021.

131 McDonald-Howard, K.-L., "Investigations into the efficacy of the slug and snail biological control *Phasmarhabditis hermaphrodita*", Liverpool John Moores University, 2023

· Barua et al. 2021 · South 1992.

133 Kosciolek, C. et al., "Toward a push–pull strategy against invasive snails using chemical and visual stimuli", *Scientific Reports*, 14 (1), 11511, 2024.

134 Forbes, E. et al., "Locomotor behaviour promotes stability of the patchy distribution of slugs in arable fields: Tracking the movement of individual *Deroceras reticulatum*", *Pest Management Science*, 76 (9), pp2944–52, 2020 · Webster, E. et al., *Gardening in a Changing Climate*, Royal Horticultural Society, 2017 · Willis, J.C. et al., "Use of an individual-based model to forecast the effect of climate change on the dynamics, abundance and geographical range of the pest slug *Deroceras reticulatum* in the UK", *Global Change Biology*, 12 (9), pp1643–57, 2006.

135 Ginn, F., "Sticky lives: slugs, detachment and more-than-human ethics in the garden", *Transactions of the Institute of British Geographers*, 39 (4), pp532–44, 2014.

Resources

BOOKS
Mc Donnell, Rory et al., *Slugs: A Guide to the Introduced and Native Fauna of California*, UCANR Publications, 2024. anrcatalog.ucanr.edu/pdf/8336.pdf

Rowson, Ben et al., *Slugs of Britain and Ireland: Identification, Understanding and Control*, Field Studies Council, 2014.

Vlach, J., *Slugs and Snails in Oregon*, Oregon Department of Agriculture Guides, 2016. oregon.gov/oda/shared/documents/publications/ippm/odaguidemolluscs2016forweb.pdf

WEBSITES
ahdb.org.uk/slugs
The Agriculture and Horticulture Development Board has collated useful slug management knowledge, although it is targeted at commercial settings.

rhs.org.uk/biodiversity/slugs-and-snails
RHS web page summarizing advice on slug and snail management, which is regularly updated as research progresses.

Terrestrial Mollusk Tool
USDA site specifically designed to assist in the identification of adult terrestrial slugs and snails of agricultural importance. idtools.org/mollusk/

INDEX

About the author

Dr. Hayley Jones leads RHS research into slugs and snails, a topic of huge interest for many gardeners. Her mission is to find effective and environmentally friendly management for plant-eating gastropods, while educating people about the gastropods' diversity and place in the garden ecosystem. Hayley shares the latest RHS research with members and the gardening public at shows and events, through the RHS Gardening Advice service, and via press interviews and television appearances.

The Royal Horticultural Society is the UK's leading gardening charity dedicated to advancing horticulture and promoting good gardening. Its charitable work includes providing expert advice and information in print, online, and at its five major gardens and annual shows, training gardeners of every age, creating hands-on opportunities for children to grow plants, and sharing research into plants, wildlife, well-being, and environmental issues affecting gardeners.

For more information visit:
www.rhs.org.uk.

Author's acknowledgments

Many thanks to Helen Griffin at RHS Publishing; Lucy Philpott and Glenda Fisher at DK and Dawn Titmus for expertly turning my words and ideas into a real-life book; and special thanks go to Amy Child for the artistic vision to bring the pages to life.

Thanks to my colleagues and collaborators, especially Imogen Cavadino and Gordon Port for their slug knowledge, enthusiasm, and shared goals in slug research, as well as my colleagues at the RHS for their support, both practical and emotional.

Finally, lots of love and appreciation to my husband, Craig, who shouldered much of the burden of moving house while I was chaotically writing to a deadline and contemplating slug facts and phrasing at all hours of the day.

Publisher's acknowledgments

Many thanks to US consultant Rory Mc Donnell, PhD. DK would also like to thank Aditya Katyal for picture research assistance, Samrajkumar S for compiling the picture credits, Katie Hewett for proofreading, Lisa Footitt for indexing, and Amy Cox for jacket concepts.

Picture credits

Penguin Random House

DK LONDON
Editorial Director Ruth O'Rourke
Project Editor Lucy Philpott
US Executive Editor Lori Cates Hand
Senior Designer Glenda Fisher
Senior Production Editor Tony Phipps
Senior Production Controller Samantha Cross
Jacket Designer Glenda Fisher
Jacket and Sales Material Coordinator Emily Cannings
Art Director Maxine Pedliham
Publishing Director Stephanie Jackson

Editorial Dawn Titmus
Design Amy Child
Illustration Ella Ginn, Dan Crisp
Jacket illustration Ella Ginn

ROYAL HORTICULTURAL SOCIETY
Consultants Simon Maughan, Chris Moncrieff, Guy Barter
Books Publisher Helen Griffin
Head of Editorial Tom Howard

First American Edition, 2025
Published in the United States by DK Publishing,
a division of Penguin Random House LLC
1745 Broadway, 20th Floor, New York, NY 10019

ISBN: 979-8-2171-2954-6

Printed and bound in China

www.dk.com